THE
COUNTRY DANCE BOOK

PARTS I & II

THE
COUNTRY DANCE BOOK

PARTS I & II

by

CECIL J. SHARP

Republished by EP Publishing Ltd., 1972
First published by Novello and Company Ltd., London

This book is a reprint of Parts I & II of "The Country Dance Book". Part I was first published in 1909; the reprint is from the 2nd edition (1934), revised and edited by Maud Karpeles. Part II was first published in 1911; the reprint is from the 3rd edition (1927). Both parts were originally published by Novello & Company Limited.

A printed list of corrections and additions, covering Parts II-VI, has been discovered. It was published by Novello & Company Limited, and is undated. The items pertaining to Parts II, III and IV are reproduced at the end of the reprint of Parts III and IV, published by EP Publishing Limited, 1975.

Republished 1972 EP Publishing Limited
East Ardsley, Wakefield
Yorkshire, England

Reprinted 1975

ISBN 0 85409 928 X

Please address all enquiries to EP Publishing Ltd.
(address as above)

Reprinted in Great Britain by
Scolar Press Limited, Ilkley, Yorkshire

THE COUNTRY DANCE BOOK

BOOK

PART I

CONTAINING A DESCRIPTION OF

EIGHTEEN TRADITIONAL DANCES ·

COLLECTED IN COUNTRY VILLAGES

BY

CECIL J. SHARP

SECOND EDITION
REVISED AND EDITED
BY

MAUD KARPELES

LONDON:
NOVELLO AND COMPANY, LIMITED

—

1934

(FIRST EDITION, 1909)
MADE IN ENGLAND

This Book is issued in connection with
" Country Dance Tunes," by the same Author

To

W. W. KETTLEWELL, ESQ.,

OF

Harptree Court, East Harptree,
Somerset

CONTENTS

PREFACE

The first edition of *The Country Dance Book*, Part 1, was published by Cecil Sharp in 1909, and during the next twelve years he published Parts 2 to 6. With a wider knowledge of the subject he evolved new and better methods of presenting the dances, and it had been his intention to revise Part 1 in order to bring the descriptions into line with the later publications. The present edition is an attempt to carry out his wishes. No changes have been made in the dances themselves, but only in the form in which they are presented.

Two new dances have been added, namely " Over the Hills to Glory," and " The Bonny Breastknot." The tune of " Over the Hills to Glory " was recorded by Cecil Sharp from Mr. William Kimber in July, 1914, and the dance-figures were recently noted from him by the editor. The version of " The Bonny Breastknot " given in the notation was recorded by the editor in Devonshire and a similar version with a slightly different tune was noted by Cecil Sharp in Somerset.

The names of certain counties have been associated with the dances, but these signify only the counties in which the dances happen to have been collected—for the Country Dances, like the folk-songs, are not peculiar to any one locality, and variants of the same dance are to be found in many different counties.

The introduction to the first edition has been reprinted practically without alteration, except that certain passages, which have a special application to the early days of the folk-dance revival, have been omitted. It should, however, be mentioned that later Cecil Sharp changed his views with regard to the origin of the Country Dance. Although it has for many generations been danced purely as a means of social and artistic recreation, Cecil Sharp believed that it had its origin in the processional and ring dances which at one time formed part of the May Day ritual.

In the original Preface Cecil Sharp acknowledges his indebtedness to Mrs. Montagu Fordham, Mrs. Stanton, Miss Wyatt-Edgell, the Rev. S. Baring-Gould, and to all those who helped him to find and note the Country Dances. He also records his thanks to Mr. William Ford, Mr. Thomas Hands, Mr. John Lavercombe, and other dancers and fiddlers from whom he obtained technical information. Thanks are also due to Miss Marjory Sinclair and Dr. Phillips Barker for the assistance they have given in reading the proofs of this revised edition.

MAUD KARPELES.

March, 1934.

INTRODUCTION

Up till a few years ago it was commonly believed that the English race was the only one in Europe that was unable to make any contribution to the literature of folk-song. Opinions may still be divided as to the artistic worth of our national folk-songs, but their existence, and in great abundance, can no longer be disputed.

A similar misconception with regard to English folk-dances awaits refutation. Maybe, the contents of this volume, following upon the issue of *The Morris Book* and other similar publications, will aid in the work of enlightenment.

In justification of the attitude of apathetic indifference which, until recently, we held towards the folk-music of our own country, it should be remembered that since the days of the Restoration the musical taste of the upper classes in England has been frankly and unashamedly cosmopolitan. This strange preference for foreign music and prejudice against the native product has been, however, characteristic only of the more educated. It has never been shared by the unlettered, who have always sung the songs and danced the dances of their forefathers, uninfluenced by, and in blissful ignorance of the habits and tastes of their more fashionable city neighbours. But this is, unhappily, no longer so. The State schools, the railways, and the hundred and one causes which have led to the depopulation of the country villages are rapidly changing, some would say debasing, the taste of the present generation—of those, that is, whose ancestors were both guardians and inventors of our traditional music and national pastimes. In the village of to-day the polka, waltz, and quadrille are steadily displacing the old-time country dances and jigs, just as the tawdry ballads and strident street-songs of the towns are no less surely exterminating the folk-songs. Fortunately, there is yet time to do for the dances what has already been done so successfully for the songs,

namely, to collect, publish, and preserve the best of them for
the benefit of our own and future generations.

But national prejudice dies hard ; more especially when it
is perpetually being nourished by those who profess to instruct.
" We cannot now find among the rural population (of England)
any traces of what may be called a national dance," says the
author of a recent *History of Dancing*—one, moreover, who
lived in the centre of that district where, perhaps, the old
dances flourish more vigorously than anywhere else in England.
A few months ago, too, the foreign correspondent of one of our
chief daily journals, after giving an account of the Northern
Games at Stockholm, innocently remarked : " It would be a
merrier and better England which could produce dances of
this kind as a spontaneous and natural growth."

This perverse indifference to facts is all the more remarkable
when we remember that in the early days of our history we
were renowned throughout Europe for our dancing no less
than for our singing.   " In saltatione et arte musicâ excellunt "
is an oft-quoted tribute paid to us by Hentzner in 1598 ; while
Beaumont spoke of the delight which the Portuguese or
Spaniards had in riding great horses, the French in courteous
behaviour, and the " dancing English in carrying a fair
presence."   But there is no need to labour the point.   The
fact that we once held this reputation is not questioned.   The
error has been too readily to assume, with our author of the
History of Dancing, that because the upper classes have for-
gotten their native songs and dances, the peasantry have been
equally neglectful.

This is especially unfortunate, for we happen to possess in
England, in the Morris and the Country Dance, two folk-
dances of unusual interest, not only to the archæologist and
student of social history, but to the lover of dancing also.
They represent two generically distinct types, of which indeed
it might be said that they differ in almost every way that one
dance can differ from another.

The Morris, for instance, is a ceremonial, spectacular, and
professional dance ; it is performed by men only, and has no
sex characteristics.

The many curious customs—as well as the extra characters,
e.g., the squire or fool, king, queen, witch, cake and sword

bearer—which are commonly associated with the dance, all indicate that the Morris was once something more than a mere dance ; that, originally, the dance formed but one part of what may very likely have been an elaborate quasi-religious ceremony. An analysis of the figures of the dance leads to the same conclusion. This may be equally true of many of the folk-dances of other nations, but very few bear upon them, as does the Morris, such clear and unmistakable indications of derivation from the primitive nature ceremonies of the early village communities.

And these qualities, which the Morris derived from its ceremonial origin, it has never lost. As practised to-day it is, as throughout its history it has always been, a formal, official dance, performed only on certain days in each year, such as Whitsun-week, the annual club feast, wake, or fair-day.

The village Morris-men, moreover, are few in number, especially chosen and trained, and form a close society or guild of professional performers. Admission into their ranks is formal and conditioned. It is not enough that the probationer should be a good dancer, lissome and agile ; he must, in addition, undergo a course of six weeks' daily instruction at the hands of the elder dancers. Upon election, he will be required to subscribe to sundry rules and regulations, and provide himself with a special and elaborate dancing dress, every detail of which, though varying from village to village, is prescribed by tradition.

The Morris, too, is remarkable for the total absence of the love motive from all its movements. There is scarcely a single dance in which the performers so much as touch each other, while " handing " is quite unknown.

Finally, it must be understood that the Morris is not, primarily, a pleasure dance. Its function is to provide a spectacle or pageant as part of the ritual associated with the celebration of popular festivals and holidays.

The Country Dance, on the other hand, possesses none of these special characteristics. It has played altogether another part in the social life of the village. No ceremony or formality has ever been associated with its performance.* It was, and

---

* *See* Preface.

so far as it is practised it still is, the ordinary, everyday dance
of the country-folk, performed not merely on festal days, but
whenever opportunity offered and the spirit of merrymaking
was abroad. So far from being a man's dance, it is performed
in couples, or partners of opposite sexes. No special dress is
needed, not even holiday clothes. The steps and figures are
simple and easily learned, so that anyone of ordinary intelli-
gence and of average physique can without difficulty qualify
as a competent performer.

Nor has the Country Dance ever been regarded as a
spectacle or pageant, like the Morris. It has always been
danced purely for its own sake, for the pleasure it afforded the
performers and the social intercourse that it provided. More
than a hundred years ago a French author drew attention to
this point in the following passage : " Au village l'on danse
pour le seul plaisir de danser, pour agiter les membres accou-
tumés à un violent exercise ; on danse pour exhaler un
sentiment de joie qui n'a pas besoin de spectateurs." The
same idea was expressed by Edward Philips, Milton's nephew,
in *The Mysteries of Love and Eloquence, or The Arte of Wooing
and Complimenting*, when he makes the dancing master say,
" Ladies, will you be pleased to dance a country dance or two,
for 'tis that which makes you truly sociable, and us truly
happy ; being like the chorus of a song where all the parts
sing together."

It is a moot point whether or not the Morris owes anything
to Moorish or other foreign influences. No such question,
however, arises with the Country Dance, which is wholly and
demonstrably English. This, it is true, has been disputed
even by English writers, who, deceived by a false etymology,
have sometimes derived it from the French *contredanse*. This
" brilliant anachronism " has been effectually refuted by
Chappell and others, by a reference to dates. They have
shown that the *contredanse* cannot be traced back further than
the seventeenth or early eighteenth centuries ; and that it is
not even mentioned by Thoinot Arbeau (1589), or by any of
the early French writers on dancing. On the other hand
Weaver, in *An Essay towards an History of Dancing* (1712),
p. 170, says, " Country dances . . . is a dancing the peculiar
growth of this nation, tho' now transplanted into almost all

the Courts of Europe ; and is become in the most august assemblies the favourite diversion. This dancing is a moderate and healthful exercise, a pleasant and innocent diversion, if modestly used and performed at convenient times, and by suitable company." Essex, too, in his *Treatise on Chorography, or the art of dancing Country Dances* (1710), writes : " This which we call Country Dancing is originally the product of this nation."

The evidence is quite conclusive. So far from deriving our Country Dances from France, it was the French who adapted one particular form of the English dance, known as " A square dance for eight," developed it, called it *contredanse*, and sent it back to England, where in the Quadrille, one of its numerous varieties, it still survives.*

Although the Country Dance originated with the unlettered classes it has not always been their exclusive possession. Just as the folk-songs were at one time freely sung by all classes of the community, so the Country Dances were once performed at Court and in fashionable ball-rooms, as well as on the village green. In the reign of James I. it was said that it was easier to put on fine clothes than to learn the French dances, and that therefore " none but Country Dances " must be used at Court. This, however, never became the invariable practice. The custom seems to have been to begin the ball with the more formal and, for the most part, foreign dances, *e.g.*, the Courante, Pavane, Gavotte, and so forth, and afterwards to indulge in the merrier and less restrained Country Dance ; just as, up to a few years ago, it was customary to finish the evening with the popular " Sir Roger."

The dances and tunes in this book have been collected in Warwickshire, Derbyshire, Devonshire, Somerset, and Surrey.† It will be noticed that, like " Sir Roger," they are all danced 'n the familiar formation of two parallel straight lines, men on one side, women on the other. This is what was called in the old dancing books " Longways for as many as will," and it is

---

* Later on, apparently, the English Quadrille came into competition with the *contredanse* in France, for " The Times " of Jan. 12, 1820, contains the following paragraph :—" It would appear that *Contredanses* are revived in Paris, to the discountenance of Quadrilles. A collection of 500 *Contredanses* are about to be published, says the Journal des Modes."

† The dances collected in Surrey had been taught by a native of Devonshire, who had settled in Surrey.

A dance collected in Oxfordshire is also included in the present edition.—M. K.

the only formation in which, apparently, the Country Dance is performed by the country folk of the present day. But this was not always so. Playford's *English Dancing Master* (1650-1728) and other similar publications contain many dances directed to be performed in other ways. There are the Rounds for " four or eight dancers " or " for as many as will " ; the " square dance for eight," already mentioned as the prototype of the Quadrille ; while in the once popular " Dargason " the performers started in a single straight line, the men and women in different groups. Many of these older dances are extremely interesting, and some of them, deciphered from the old dancing books, will be described in the second part of this work.

CECIL SHARP.

1909.

TECHNICAL TERMS AND SYMBOLS

◯=man ; ▢=woman.

The *Set* or the *General Set* is the area occupied or enclosed by the dancers.

The *Presence* is the top of the room, *i.e.*, the end nearest the music.

To *cross hands*, the man takes the right and left hand of his partner with his right and left hand respectively, the right hands being uppermost.

The term *lead* is used when partners move with joined hands.

To *move* is to dance forwards.

To move *up* or *down* is to move toward the top or the bottom of the room.

To *fall back* is to dance backwards.

To pass *by the right* is to pass right shoulder to right shoulder ; *by the left*, left shoulder to left shoulder.

To *cast off* is to turn outward and dance outside the General Set.

To *cast up* or *cast down* is to turn outward (unless already so facing) and dance up or down outside the General Set.

The term *clockwise* (cl.) or *counter-clockwise* (c.cl.) are self-explanatory, and refer to the direction of circular movements.

To make a *half-turn* is to turn through half a circle so as to face in an opposite direction ; to make a *whole-turn* is to make a complete revolution.

r.=a step taken with the right foot ; l.=a step taken with the left foot.

h.r.=a hop on to the right foot ; h.l.=a hop on to the left foot.

This figure can, if preferred, be replaced by the next one. When this is done the Swing (a non-progressive figure) must take the place of the Swing and change.

FIRST COUPLE LEADS DOWN THE MIDDLE AND BACK AND CASTS
ONE PLACE

The first four bars are performed as in the preceding figure. During the next four bars, first man and first woman lead back to places with right hands, or crossed hands ; then, releasing hands, they cast off round second man and second woman, respectively, into second couple's place, whilst second couple moves up into first couple's place. This is a progressive figure.

FORMATION

The dances in this volume are all of the *longways for as many as will* formation and can be performed by any equal numbers of men and women, not fewer than eight in all (or ten, in a triple minor-set dance, see p. 18).   The performers take partners and stand in two parallel lines, the men on one side facing the women on the other, each dancer standing opposite his or her partner.   This formation is depicted in the following diagram :

RIGHT WALL
(WOMEN'S SIDE)

TOP   □ □ □ □ · · · · □   BOTTOM

      ○ ○ ○ ○ · · · · ○

LEFT WALL
(MEN'S SIDE)

The distance between the lines should be approximately five feet, and between the couples about two and a half feet.

PROGRESSION IN A LONGWAYS DANCE

A *progressive longways* dance consists of an indefinite number of repetitions of a series of figures, which vary both in number and character in different dances. This series of figures is called the *complete figure*. Each performance of the complete figure is called a *round*. Every complete figure must contain, *inter alia*, what is called a *progressive figure*, the effect of which is to change the order and position of some or all of the couples. Consequently, as the dance proceeds, the couples are continually changing places, in an ordered way, some moving up and others down the General Set.

In the notation the figures of one complete round will be described, and these are to be repeated in the new positions, without pause, as often as is desired. At the end of the last round partners honour each other (see p. 28.)

There are two ways in which the progressive movement is effected, giving rise to two different types of dance : the *whole-set* and the *minor-set* dance.

THE WHOLE-SET DANCE

In dances of this species the progressive movement is effected by the transference of the first couple from the top to the bottom of the General Set. With every round, therefore, each couple (with the exception of the one at the top) moves up one place, and continues this movement, step by step, until it reaches the top of the General Set, when, after the next round, it is transferred to the bottom, to resume once again its upward progress. " Sir Roger de Coverley " is a good example of this type of dance.

The top couple is called the *leading couple*.

Country Dance Book—Part I.—Revised Ed.—Novello—B

THE MINOR-SET DANCE

In a minor-set dance the figures are performed simultaneously by subsidiary sets, *i.e.*, groups of two, or three, adjacent couples. The progressive figure is invariably performed by the first and second of these couples, and results in the transposition of their respective positions.

These subsidiary groups of dancers are called *minor-sets—duple* or *triple* according to the number of couples they contain. The several couples of a duple minor-set are called, counting from the top, first and second, respectively, and of a triple minor-set, *first, second* and *third* respectively.

Of these, the first is the leading couple. It moves one place down the General Set every round, and becomes the first couple of a new minor-set in the following round. The function of the second and third couples is to aid the first one in the performance of the several figures.

A couple that is not attached to any minor-set throughout a complete round, and is therefore not engaged in the performance of that round, is called a *neutral* couple.

The progression in a *duple minor-set* dance is effected by the upper (first) and lower (second) couples of each minor-set changing places, the former moving down one place, the latter up. This will result in a rearrangement of the minor-sets in the following Round, in which each upper couple will make a new minor-set with the couple immediately below, or—to put it in another way—each lower couple will make a new minor-set by dancing with the couple immediately above. In this way every couple, as the dance proceeds, will move steadily from one end of the Set to the other, the upper couples down, the lower ones up. Every couple upon reaching either end of the Set must remain *neutral* during the next round, after which it will again enter the dance and progress in the direction opposite to that in which it had previously been moving (upper couples becoming lower couples, and vice versa).

In the *triple minor-set* dance, the first or leading couple moves down the General Set, whilst the second and third couples move up. The progression is effected by the first couple changing places with the second. Thus in the next Round the first couple will be the leading couple of the two couples immediately below it; the second couple will dance, as third couple, with the two couples above it; and the third couple will take the part of the second couple. It will thus be seen that the first or leading couple moves down one place in each round, whilst those coming up the dance, who alternately take the part of the second and third couples, move up only in every other round.

When the leading couple reaches the couple at the bottom of the Set, the two couples together may perform as much of the Complete Figure as is practicable, and they must in any case change places. After this last change the leading couple will remain neutral for one round at the bottom of the Set, after which it will proceed to move up the dance as, alternately, third and second couple.

On reaching the top of the dance, or the top place but one, the couples must remain neutral (and must not change places) until three couples are available to form a minor-set. A couple on reaching the top of the dance will therefore have to remain neutral for two rounds.

The principle of the triple minor progression can be seen in the following diagram. Neutral couples are placed between parentheses and minor-sets within square brackets. The symbol <—> is placed between the two couples who make the progression by changing places.

[A <—> B   C]   [D <—> E   F]

(B)   [A <—> C   E]   [D <—> F]

(B)   (C)   [A <—> E   F]   (D)

[B <—> C   E]   [A <—> F   D]

Amongst traditional dancers it is customary for the dance, whether duple minor or triple minor, to be started by the top minor-set only, and for the rest of the dancers to remain neutral until the leading couple reaches them.

STEPS AND MOTION

The Country Dance is pre-eminently a figure dance, depending in the main for its expressiveness upon the weaving of patterned, concerted evolutions rather than upon intricate steps or elaborate body-movements.

The steps used in the traditional Country Dance are few in number and simple in execution. When, in its later developments, the dance became popular in polite society, the usual steps, *e.g.*, the chassé, assemblé, jetté, &c., were used and taught by the fashionable dancing masters. But these steps do not properly belong to the traditional dance, though possibly they may originally have been derived therefrom. Country folk never point the toe, arch the leg, attitudinize, or affect a swaying or mincing gait. Movements of this kind are quite alien to the spirit of the Country Dance, which is one of gaiety and simple good humour rather than of conventional elegance.

An analysis of the way in which the traditional folk-dancer moves shows that it is based upon two main principles :

1. The weight of the body in motion must always be supported wholly on one foot or the other, and never carried on both feet at the same moment. From this it follows that the transition from step to step, *i.e.*, the transference of the weight from one foot to the other, must always be effected by spring.

2. The motive force, although derived in part from this foot-spring, is also due to the action of gravity, brought into play by the inclination of the body from the vertical. The dancer in motion is always in unstable equilibrium, regulating both the speed and the direction of his movement by varying the poise and balance of his body. When moving along the straight, for instance, his body will be poised either in front of his feet or behind them, according

as his movement is forward or backward ; and laterally when moving along a curved track. In other words, the foot must not take the ground in advance of the body. The function of the legs is to support the body rather then to help to move it forward, the actual motion being set up, regulated, and directed by the sway and balance of the body, as in skating. The body, it should be pointed out, cannot be used in this way, that is to set up and regulate motion, unless it is carried essentially in line from head to foot, without bend at the neck or at the waist, or sag at the knees.

The advantages of this way of moving are obvious. Motion is started and kept up with the least expenditure of muscular energy ; it can be regulated, both as to speed and direction, with the greatest ease and nicety ; above all, its expressive value is high in that it brings the whole body, and not the legs alone, into play. This last consideration is a weighty one. The strongest argument against " leg-dancing " is not merely that it is ugly, or that it involves superfluous muscular effort, but that the legs, being primarily concerned and almost wholly occupied in supporting and preserving the equilibrium of the body, cannot effectively be employed for expressive or any other purpose.

The following general directions apply to the execution of all the steps used in the Country Dance :

1. There are normally two steps to each bar, which fall on the main divisions of the bar, whether the time be simple or compound. In the case of a compound step, that is, one that comprises more than one movement, the accented movement should fall on the beat.

2. The step should fall on the ball of the foot, not on the toe, with the heel off, but close to, the ground.

3. The feet should be held straight and parallel, neither turned out nor in at the ankle.

4. The legs should never be straddled, but held close together. Nor again should they be extended more than is absolutely necessary ; for the movement should, as far as possible, be made by spring and not by stride.

5. The jar caused by the impact of the foot on the floor should be absorbed mainly by the ankle-joint, and very little by the knee. The knee should be bent as little as possible, so little that the supporting leg should appear to be straight, *i.e.*, in one line from hip to ankle.

6. All unnecessary movements should be suppressed, *e.g.*, kicking up the heels, fussing with the feet, raising the knees, etc.

In the notation specific steps are in most cases prescribed, but these are not to be regarded as obligatory, and it should be remembered that it is not necessary for every dancer to use the same step at the same time, nor for a figure to be danced throughout with the same step.

Where alternative steps are given in the notation, the roman type indicates the steps which were used by traditional dancers, and the italicised type signifies those which have become customary during the practice of recent years.

WALKING-STEP (W.S.)

This is the normal step of the traditional Country Dance. It is executed in accordance with the above instructions and with more spring than in an ordinary walking-step. Although both feet may touch the ground at the same time, the weight of the body must always be supported wholly on one foot or on the other.

RUNNING-STEP (R.S.)

This is an ordinary running-step, executed neatly and lightly. The spring should not be exaggerated, but should be sufficiently high for both feet to be off the ground during the transition from step to step. The difference between this and the walking-step is one of degree rather than of kind and the distinction lies in the amount of spring. This cannot be stereotyped, but must depend upon the character of the dance, the mood of the dancer, and the relation of the step to the dance-phrase. In practice it will be found that a gradual transition from running-step to walking-step or vice versa, will often be made during the course of a single figure.

SKIPPING-STEP (sk.s.)

This is the usual step and hop on alternate feet.   The accent is on the step, which must fall, therefore, on the beat.   The rhythm of the step is as follows :

r.   h.r.   l.   h.l.   r.   h.r.   l   h.l

That is to say, the duration of the step is twice as long as that of the hop.   Care should be taken not to stride, and to travel on the hop as well as on the step.

HOP-STEP (h.s.)

This is the same as the skipping-step, but is performed in even rhythm, as follows :

r.   h.r.   l.   h.l.   r.   h.r.   l.   h.l.

SLIPPING-STEP (sl.s.)

This is a series of springs, made sideways, with alternate feet, the major spring being made off the leading foot, *i.e.*, the left when going to the left and the right when going to the right. Although the legs are thus alternately opening and closing, scissor-fashion, the motion is effected almost wholly by the spring, and not the straddle ;   the legs, therefore, should be separated as little as possible.   The free foot should not be allowed to scrape the ground.

The accent falls on the foot off which the major spring is made, that is, the left or right, according to the direction of motion, thus :

Moving to the left.

l. r. l. r. l. r. l. r.

Moving to the right.

r. l. r. l. r. l. r. l.

SIDEWAYS-STEP (si.s.)

This is the same as the slipping-step, but is performed in even rhythm, as follows :

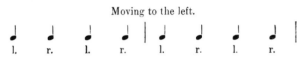

Moving to the left.

l. r. l. r. l. r. l. r.

CHANGE-HOP STEP (ch.h.s.)

This step consists of three steps on alternate feet followed by a hop on the same foot (four steps to the bar). The rhythm of the step is as follows :

$\frac{4}{4}$ r. l. r. h.r. l. r. l. h.l.

or

$\frac{6}{8}$ r. l. r. h.r. l. r. l. h.l.

There should be a slight spring on each step, the amount varying according to the character of the dance, but the movement should be continuous and the weight of the body should be kept over the supporting foot. On the second step of the bar, the foot should normally take the ground either side by side with the other foot or immediately behind it.

CHANGE-STEP (ch.s.)

This is performed in the same way as the preceding step, but omitting the hop, *i.e.*

or

ARMS AND HANDS

Nearly all the prescribed arm-movements in the Country Dance relate to the joining of hands. Of ornamental or fanciful movements there are none, nor any of formal design that are devised—like many of the arm-movements of the Morris Dance—to assist the actions of the dancer. Nevertheless, perhaps for this reason, the carriage and manipulation of the hands and arms form a very characteristic feature of the Country Dance.

It may be taken as a general rule that when the arms are not in active use, *i.e.*, when they are not being directly employed for some specific purpose, they should be allowed to swing quietly and loosely by the side. This involves complete relaxation of the muscles that control the shoulder, elbow, and wrist joints, and the capacity to resist sympathetic, involuntary tension in other muscles.

The dancer may sometimes find it necessary to make use of his arms to maintain his balance, *e.g.*, to throw out the outside arm when moving swiftly round a sharp curve. This is permissible, provided that such movements are made only when really necessary, simply, and without exaggeration.

All the prescribed hand and arm movements in the Country Dance have a definite purpose, and in their execution no more is required of the dancer than that he should fulfil this purpose effectively and in the simplest and most direct way. For instance, in " leading " the taking of hands is not a mere formality ; the dancer should actually lead—that is, support his partner, guide and regulate her movement.

In linking right hand with right, or left with left, the hands are held sideways (*i.e.*, in a vertical plane), thumbs uppermost, and brought lightly together, not clenched, the four fingers of each hand resting on the palm of the other, and the thumb pressing on the knuckle of the middle finger. The hands should be joined in this manner in leading, and in turning with one hand.

In joining inside hands, that is, right hand with left, or left hand with right, *e.g.*, in rings, turning with both hands, &c., the man holds his hand palm upward, the woman places her hand in his, and the fingers are clasped as before.

When two men or two women join inside hands, it is suggested that the dancer having the lower number should always take the man's position (*i.e.* give his hand palm upward).

MOVEMENTS AND FIGURES

The number of figures that are known to have been used at one time or another in the history of the Country Dance is very large ; and this means that the number of possible varieties of the Country Dance is practically infinite. For any series of figures, combined in accordance with the theory of the dance and in conformity with the structure of the tune, will constitute a complete figure. With two exceptions, " The Triumph " and " Sir Roger de Coverley," each of which is invariably danced in its own way and to its own tune, not a single one of the innumerable varieties of the Country Dance has ever been recognised, except locally, as a fixed and distinct dance.

It should be mentioned that when the Country Dance was performed in the ball-room it was the custom for the leading couple to have the " call," that is, the privilege of naming the tune and prescribing the figures. It was necessary, therefore, for expert dancers of those days to be proficient not only in the performance of the dance but in the theory as well. For the benefit of those who were unable to make the " call " numerous publications were issued from the 17th century onwards, containing Country Dance airs, together with the descriptions of the figures, though not of the steps that were to be danced to them. Similar descriptions, but with the names only of the tunes to which they were to be performed, were also often printed on the fly-leaves of pocket-books and diaries of the 18th and early 19th centuries. Usually, though not invariably, the name of the dance was derived from thav of the tune.

The figures tabulated in the notation follow one another without pause.

THE HONOUR

This is a formal obeisance made by partners to one anothei at the conclusion, and sometimes in the course, of the dance.

The man bows, and the woman makes a slight curtsey or " bob."

The honour should always be made in rhythm with the music and when it occurs at the conclusion of the dance there should, if possible, be some corresponding movement of the feet. The exact way in which this is done depends upon circumstances. The usual method is to place the right foot on the ground twelve inches or so to the side, say, on the first beat of the bar, and to bring up the left foot beside it—or, in the case of the woman, behind it—on the following beat when the obeisance is made.

Amongst traditional dancers it is often customary for partners to honour each other before the dance begins as well as at the conclusion of the dance.

THE BALANCE

Two dancers face. They step on the right foot at the beginning of the bar, and on the second beat of the bar they hop on the right foot, and swing the left foot across in front of the right leg. In the second bar the movement is repeated on the left foot, swinging the right foot across. The movement can also be started on the left foot.

THE TURN

Two dancers face each other, join both hands (unless otherwise stated) with arms outstretched, swing round once clockwise, separate and fall back to places. The dancers should face each other throughout the movement, keep their arms extended, and lean back slightly so as to support each other's weight. When the turn is performed with one hand, dancers stand sideways to each other and face in opposite directions.

THE SWING

This is the same as the turn with both hands, except that the dancers swing round more than once before separating.

Traditional dancers of the present day engage their partners in waltz fashion, but the older method, which dropped out of fashion owing to the influence of the Waltz and Polka, was to take hands as described in the Turn.   It is suggested that the older method be adhered to.

SWING AND CHANGE

Two couples swing, as above described, and at the same time they change places by revolving round each other in a half-circle clockwise.   This is a progressive figure.

ARM WITH THE RIGHT (OR LEFT)

Two performers, usually partners, meet, link right (or left) arms, swing round a complete circle, clockwise (or counter-clockwise), separate, and fall back to places (r.s.).

In order that the dancers may give and receive mutual support in the execution of the whole turn, the arms, crooked at right angles, must be linked at the elbows, the dancers leaning slightly away from each other.

RIGHT (OR LEFT) HANDS-ACROSS

This is performed by four dancers standing in a square. Each dancer joins right (or left) hands with the dancer diagonally opposite.   Holding their hands close together, chin-high, all dance round clockwise (or counter-clockwise).

HANDS-THREE, HANDS-FOUR, ETC.

Three or more dancers, as directed, form a ring, extend arms, join hands a little above waist-level, and dance round.   In the absence of specific instructions to the contrary it is to be understood that one complete circuit is to be danced, clockwise, the performers facing centre.

The dancers should clasp hands firmly, lean slightly outward, and thus support each other.   When the movement is followed by a repetition in the reverse direction, counter-clockwise, the dancers may stamp on the first step of the second movement.

THE TURN SINGLE

The dancer makes a whole turn on his axis, clockwise (unless otherwise directed), taking four low springing steps with alternate feet, beginning with the right foot. The body must be held erect, and the turn regulated so that the dancer completes the circle and regains his original position on the last step.

THE DOUBLE

This is performed by taking three steps (w.s. or r.s.) forward or backward, followed by a closing of the feet, *i.e.*, four steps, the last of which is made in position (*i.e.*, feet together), the weight of the body being supported either on one foot or on both feet, according to circumstances. Sometimes, *e.g.*, in " Over the Hills to Glory " (see p. 43), instead of the fourth step, a very slight hop is made and the free foot is swung slightly forward (or back when the movement is backward).

FIRST COUPLE LEADS DOWN THE MIDDLE AND BACK

First man leads his partner with the right hand down the middle of the Set. Raising their joined hands, the man turns his partner under his right arm, half-way round counter-clockwise, whilst he also makes a half-turn counter-clockwise, and they both face up (4 bars). First man leads his partner back to the top of the Set with right hands, or crossed hands. They release hands and fall back into their own places, some-times concluding by bowing to each other (4 bars). When they slip back, partners should face and take both hands:

An alternative method of performing this figure is for partners to lead down either with left, or right hands, turn inwards towards each other, and either lead back with right hands, or else slip (sl.s. or si.s.) back, facing each other and holding both hands.

NOTATION

——— ———

BRIGHTON CAMP

(Devonshire)

MUSIC		MOVEMENTS
		WHOLE-SET
A*		All face up, and partners cross hands. First couple, followed by the other couples, casts off to the left, dances down to the bottom of the Set, turns to the left and dances up the middle to position (ch.h.s. or *sk.s.*).
B1	1-8	Partners face, and first couple swings down the middle to the lowest place (ch.h.s. or *sk.s.*); while all the other couples move up one place (progressive).
B2	1-8	All couples swing (ch.h.s. or *sk.s.*).
		* *When many couples are dancing it may be necessary to repeat the music to this figure.*

GALOPEDE

(Warwickshire)

MUSIC	MOVEMENTS
	WHOLE-SET
A1 1-4	Women take hands; and men take hands, or link arms. All move forward a double, partners honouring each other on the first beat of the second bar, and fall back a double to places (w.s.).
5-8	Release hands and partners change places, passing each other by the right (w.s.).
A2	Movement as in A1 repeated to places.
B	All couples swing (ch.s. or *sk.s.*).
C	First couple swings down the middle to the lowest place (ch.s.or *sk.s.*) ; while all the other couples move up one place (progressive).

RIBBON DANCE

(Derbyshire and Surrey)

MUSIC	MOVEMENTS
	WHOLE-SET
A 1-2	Partners hold a ribbon between them in their right hands.
	First and second, third and fourth, fifth and sixth couples, &c., face each other and change places, the first, third, and fifth couples raising right arms and passing ribbons over the heads of second, fourth, and sixth couples (w.s.).
3-4	Movement repeated to places, second, fourth, and sixth couples passing ribbons over the heads of first, third, and fifth couples (w.s.).
5-8	As in bars 1-4.
	If the number of couples is uneven, the last couple will be neutral during this figure.
B1*	First man and first woman separate and cast off, followed by all the other men and women except the last couple. Partners meet below the last couple, pass successively under an arch made by the last couple, move up the middle and return to their respective places (h.s. or *sk.s.*).
	Each woman should release her end of the ribbon, and throw it to her partner as she casts off, and then take it again as she meets her partner and passes under the arch.

RIBBON DANCE—*continued.*

MUSIC	MOVEMENTS
B2	First couple swings down the middle under arches made by all the other couples to the lowest place (h.s. or *sk.s.*) ; while all the other couples move up one place (progressive).
	The last Round ends with the cast off figure (B1), which is varied in the following way. The first man and the first woman, after passing under the arch, instead of proceeding to the top of the General Set, place themselves next to the last couple, and make an arch with their ribbon. The second couple then passes under the two arches, takes up a position next to the first couple, and makes an arch. The remaining couples follow suit.
	* *When many couples are dancing it may be necessary to repeat the music to this figure.*

THE BUTTERFLY

(Warwickshire)

MUSIC	MOVEMENTS
	DUPLE MINOR-SET
A1 1-4	First and second couples right-hands-across (*w.s.*).
5-8	First and second couples left-hands-across.
B 1-4	Partners take right hands. First and second couples face, and first couple moves down a double, holding up right hands to make an arch ; whilst second couple moves up, passing under the arch made by first couple. All face in the opposite direction and move a double back to places, first couple passing under the arch made by second couple (*w.s.*).
5-8	As in B 1-4.
A2	First and second couples swing and change (ch.s. or *sk.s.*).
	Traditionally it is customary for partners to hold between them a handkerchief, or two handkerchiefs knotted together, with which they form the arch.

WE WON'T GO HOME TILL MORNING

(Warwickshire)

MUSIC	MOVEMENTS
	WHOLE-SET
A1 1-4	First and second couples right-hands-across (sk.s. or r.s.).
5-8	First and second couples left-hands-across (sk.s. or r.s.).
B1	All stand still, facing partners, and dancers clap their hands in the following rhythm :
	$\begin{array}{l}6 \\ 8\end{array}$ ♩. ♩. | ♩. | ♩. ♩. | ♩. |
A2	First couple leads down the middle (w.s) and back and casts one place (sk.s.).
B2	As in B1.
A3	Partners swing (sk.s.).

SPEED THE PLOUGH

(Surrey)

MUSIC	MOVEMENTS
	DUPLE MINOR-SET
A1 1-4	First man leads first woman down four steps towards second woman. On the first beat of the third bar, first couple and second woman honour ; and first couple then falls back a little way (w.s.).
5-8	As in bars 1-4 with second man.
A2	The first couple leads down the middle (w.s.) and back (si.s.).
B1 1-4	Partners cross over left shoulders into opposite places and make a half-turn clockwise (w.s.).
5-8	Partners cross over right shoulders and make a half-turn counter-clockwise (w.s.).
B2	First and second couples swing and change (ch.h.s.)

POP GOES THE WEASEL

(First version)

Longways for as many as will

(Warwickshire)

MUSIC	MOVEMENTS
	DUPLE MINOR-SET
A1 1-6	First man and first and second women hands-three once-and-a-half round clockwise (sl.s.).
7-8	First man and second woman stand still and hold up inside hands, making an arch, whilst first woman " pops under " to her place (r.s.).
A2 1-6	Without releasing hands, first man and second woman go hands-three with second man once-and-a-half round clockwise (sl.s.).
7-8	Second man " pops under " the arch made by first man and second woman (r.s.).
B1	First couple leads down the middle (w.s.) and back again (sl.s. or *sk.s.*)
B2	First and second couples swing and change (ch.s. or *sk.s.*).

POP GOES THE WEASEL

(Second version)

(Warwickshire)

MUSIC	MOVEMENTS
	DUPLE MINOR-SET
A1 1-6	First man and first woman turn with right hands twice round (sk.s.).
7-8	First man and first woman raise their right hands, making an arch. Second woman passes under (*i.e.*, " pops ") into first woman's place (r.s.).
A2	As in A1, second man passing under the arch into first man's place (progressive).
B1	First couple leads down the middle (w.s.) and back again into the second couple's place (sk.s.).
B2	First and second couples swing (sk.s.).

THE FLOWERS OF EDINBURGH

(Warwickshire)

MUSIC	MOVEMENTS
	DUPLE MINOR-SET
A1	First man goes the Figure-8 round the second couple, *i.e.*, he passes counter-clockwise round second woman and clockwise round second man and returns to his place (ch.s., *ch.h.s.*, or *sk.s.*).
A2	First woman goes the Figure-8 round the second couple, passing clockwise round second man and counter-clockwise round second woman.
B1	First man and first woman simultaneously go the Figure-8 round second couple, first woman passing in front of her partner.
B2	First and second couples swing and change (ch.s., *ch.h.s.*, or *sk.s.*) (progressive).

OVER THE HILLS TO GLORY

(Oxfordshire)

MUSIC	MOVEMENTS
	DUPLE MINOR-SET
A1 1-4	First and second men lead forward a double and back with inside hands, whilst the two women do the same (*see* p. 31).
5-6	First and second men lead forward a double, whilst the women do the same.
7-8	All fall back to places, turning single outwards as they do so, *i.e.*, first man and second woman counter-clockwise, and first woman and second man clockwise.
A2	As in A1.
B1 1-6	First man with his right hand leads his partner down the middle of the Set. They make a half-turn inwards towards each other and lead back into the second couple's place (w.s.), whilst the second couple moves up into the first couple's place (progressive).
7-8	First and second men turn their partners once round (h.s.).
B2	As in B1, second couple leading down the middle and back into first place.
	N.B.—*Neutral couples join in the turn in bars* **7** *and* 8 *of B*1 *and B*2.

NANCY'S FANCY

(Devonshire)

MUSIC	MOVEMENTS
	DUPLE MINOR-SET
A* 1-4	First and second men move forward a double and back; simultaneously first and second women join right hands and move forward a double and back, passing between the two men (w.s. or *r.s.*).
5-8	Movement repeated, the two men joining right hands and passing between the two women.
B	First couple leads down the middle (w.s.) and back and casts one place (ch.s. or *sk.s.*) (progressive).
C	First and second couples swing (ch.s. or *sk.s.*)
	* An alternative figure for A music is hands-four clockwise, and counter-clockwise.

BONNETS SO BLUE, or CROSS HANDS

(Warwickshire)

MUSIC		MOVEMENTS
		DUPLE MINOR-SET
A	1-4	First and second couples right-hands-across (sk.s.).
	5-8	First and second couples left-hands-across (sk.s.).
B		First couple leads down the middle (w.s.) and back and casts one place (sk.s.).
C		First and second couples swing (sk.s.).

THE TRIUMPH

(Surrey)

MUSIC	MOVEMENTS
	TRIPLE MINOR-SET*
A1 1-4	Second man takes first woman by the left hand and leads her down the middle, whilst first man crosses over and casts down below third woman and meets his partner in the middle of the set (w.s.).
5-8	The three dancers face up in line, second man being on the left of first woman and first man on her right. First woman, still holding second man's left hand, gives her right hand to first man, and he joins his left hand with the right hand of the second man, thus making an arch over first woman's head. In this position the first and second men lead the first woman back up the middle, " in triumph," to her place.
A2	As in A1, first man leading second woman down the middle, whilst second man crosses over and casts down.
B	First couple leads down the middle (w.s.) and back (h.s. or *ch.h.s.*).
C	First and second couples swing and change (h.s. or *ch.h.s.*).
	* *This dance can, if desired, be performed as a duple minor-set dance.*

STEP AND FETCH HER. or FOLLOW YOUR LOVER

(Devonshire)

MUSIC	MOVEMENTS
	TRIPLE MINOR-SET*
A1	Second man leads first woman down the middle, whilst first man crosses over and casts down below third woman. First man displaces second man, crosses hands with his partner and leads her up the middle, while second man follows behind, and all return to places (w.s.).
A2	As above, first man leading second woman down the middle, whilst second man crosses over and casts down, &c.
B	First couple leads down the middle (w.s.) and back (h.s.).
C	First and second couples swing and change (h.s.).
	* This dance can, if desired, be performed as a duple minor-set dance.

HASTE TO THE WEDDING
(First version)

(Surrey)

MUSIC	MOVEMENTS
	TRIPLE MINOR-SET*
A1 1-4	First man casts down, whilst first woman moves down the middle (w.s.).
5-8	First man and first woman fall back to places, turning single and raising both arms above their heads in bars 7 and 8.
A2 1-4	First man moves down the middle, whilst first woman casts down.
5-8	First man and first woman fall back to places.
B1	First couple leads down the middle (w.s.) and back (sl.s. or *sk.s.*).
B2	First and second couples swing and change (ch.s. or *sk.s.*).
	* *This dance can, if desired, be performed as a duple minor-set dance.*

HASTE TO THE WEDDING
(Second Version)

(Devonshire)

Longways for as many as will

MUSIC	MOVEMENTS
	DUPLE MINOR-SET
A1	First man and second woman move forward a double and meet (w.s.), honouring each other on the first beat of the second bar (2 bars), cast back to places (2 bars), and turn each other (4 bars) (w.s. or *r.s.*).
A2	Movement repeated by first woman and second man.
B1	First couple leads down the middle (w.s.) and back (sl.s. or *sk.s.*).
B2	First and second couples swing and change (ch.s. or *sk.s.*).

HUNT THE SQUIRREL

(Surrey)

MUSIC	MOVEMENTS
	TRIPLE MINOR-SET
A1 1-4	First and second couples hands-four clockwise (w.s.).
5-8	First and second couples hands-four counter-clockwise (w.s.).
B1	First man and first woman cast off below third couple and lead up the middle with right hands into second couple's place, whilst second man and second woman move up into first couple's place, take right hands and face down to meet first couple (w.s.).
A2 1-4	Second and first couples, facing each other, lead down the middle, first couple falling backwards (w.s.).
5-8	Second and first couples, still facing, move up the middle. Second man and second woman, on reaching their places, make an arch under which first couple passes (h.s.).
B2	First and second couples swing and change (h.s.) (progressive).

TINK A TINK

(Surrey)

MUSIC	MOVEMENTS
	TRIPLE MINOR-SET*
A1 1-4	First and second couples arm right (h.s. or *w.s.*).
5-8	First and second couples arm left.
B	First couple leads down the middle (h.s. or *w.s.*). First man casts off round third man and returns to his place ; whilst his partner casts off round third woman and returns to her place (h.s.).
A2	First and second couples hands-four clockwise (4 bars) and counter-clockwise (4 bars) (h.s. or *w.s.*).
C	First and second couples swing and change (h.s. or *ch.h.s.*) (progressive).
	* *This dance can, if desired, be performed as a duple minor-set dance.*

THREE MEET, or THE PLEASURES OF THE TOWN

(Devonshire)

MUSIC	MOVEMENTS
	TRIPLE MINOR-SET
A1	The three men link arms and the three women link arms, and all move forward a double to partners and back twice (w.s.).
A2	Partners cross hands, and first couple, followed by second and third couples, casts off to the left and returns up the middle to place (sk.s.).*
B1	First couple leads down the middle (w.s.) and back and casts one place (sk.s.) (progressive).
B2	First and second couples swing (sk.s.).
	* *An alternative version of this figure is for all the couples to follow the top couple as in a whole-set dance.*

THE BONNY BREASTKNOT

(Somerset and Devonshire)

MUSIC	MOVEMENTS
	TRIPLE MINOR-SET
A1 1-4	First man leads his partner with right hand between second and third woman, and they cast off, first man round third woman, and first woman round second woman (w.s. or r.s.).
5-8	Not taking hands, first couple passes between second and third men, and first man casts off round third man, whilst first woman casts off round second man (w.s. or r.s.).
B1 1-4	First woman stands between second man and second woman, and all three take hands, facing down ; meanwhile first man stands between third man and third woman, and all three take hands, facing up. In this position all balance, starting with left foot (*see* p. 29), and repeat.
5-8	First woman stands between second and third women ; whilst first man stands between second and third men. They take hands and, facing partners, balance as before (progressive).

THE BONNY BREASTKNOT—*continued*

MUSIC	MOVEMENTS
A2 1-4	First man arms right with his partner half-way round. First man then arms left with third woman, whilst first woman arms left with second man (w.s. or r.s.).
5-8	First man arms right with his partner three-quarters round. First man then arms left with second woman, whilst first woman arms left with third man (w.s. or r.s.).
B2 1-4	First man (who is now on the women's side) takes his partner with right hand and they slip down the middle.
5-8	First man slips back with his partner, turns her rather more than once round, so that they finish in position to start the next round.

The English Dancing Master:

OR,

Plaine and easie Rules for the Dancing of Country Dances, with the Tune to each Dance.

march. 19th

LONDON,

Printed by *Thomas Harper*, and are to be sold by *John Playford*, at his Shop in the Inner Temple neere the Church doore. 1651 1660

THE

COUNTRY DANCE BOOK

PART II.

CONTAINING

THIRTY COUNTRY DANCES

FROM

THE ENGLISH DANCING MASTER
(1650—1728)

DESCRIBED BY

CECIL J. SHARP.

FIRST EDITION, 1911.
SECOND EDITION, 1913.
THIRD EDITION, 1927.

LONDON:

NOVELLO AND COMPANY, Ltd.

1927

MADE IN ENGLAND

This Book is issued in connection with " Country Dance Tunes,"
by the same Author.

CONTENTS.

THE ILLUSTRATIONS.

Frontispiece: Title-page of "The English Dancing Master."

The copy in the British Museum, from which this reproduction was made, is one of the Thomason Tracts (1640-61), a collection of some 32,000 pamphlets in 2,000 volumes, presented to the nation by George III., in 1762. Carlyle considered these tracts "to be the most valuable set of documents connected with English history; greatly preferable to all the sheep-skins in the Tower and other places, for informing the English what the English were in former times."

The altered date "March 19th, 1650" (*i.e.*, O.S.) is in the handwriting of the collector, Thomason, and probably records the date of purchase.

The book was entered at Stationers' Hall "7 Novembris 1650," rather more than four months before Thomason acquired his copy. The engraving is by Wenceslaus Hollar (1607-77), the Bohemian etcher.

Plate facing page 72: Tune and notation of "Newcastle" (1st ed., 1650).

The crescents and circles in the diagram represent the men and women respectively. In the third and subsequent editions the meaning of these symbols was reversed, the circles representing the men, the crescents the women.

The abbreviations are thus explained by Playford: Wo. = woman ; We. = women ; Co. = contrary ; S. = single ; D. = double ; 1, 2, 3, etc. = first, second, third, etc.; $\underline{\bullet}$ = a strain of the tune once over ; $\underline{:}$ = a strain of the tune twice over.

The wording of the notation to the second strain of the second Part is very perplexing. The only way I can make sense of it is by omitting the first comma (after "meet").

Plate facing page 13: Tune and notation of "Parson's Farewell" (3rd ed., 1665).

Comparing the tune with the original version in the first edition (see "Country Dance Tunes," Set 3, p. 1) it will be seen that (1) a bar is omitted in the second strain; (2) certain auxiliary notes have been added in the penultimate bars of each strain; and (3) the seventh note of the scale has been raised a semitone.

There is clearly a misprint in the diagram; the first woman should face down, not up.

In the text I have altered the positions of the couples, placing them sideways to the audience instead of back and face. This does not, of course, affect any of the movements.

INTRODUCTION.

THE first edition of "The English Dancing Master, or plaine and easie Rules for the Dancing of Country Dances, with the tune to each dance" (104 dances; oblong 4to), is dated 1651, but was entered at Stationers' Hall in the preceding year.

With an altered title—"The Dancing Master"—and in a slightly different shape—oblong 12mo—a second edition, "enlarged and corrected from many grosse errors which were in the former edition" (112 dances), was issued in 1652. The book went through seventeen editions, the last being issued in three parts, the first (358 dances) in 1721, and the second (360 dances) and the third (200 dances) in 1728. During this period of seventy-eight years the book passed through many changes. Many of the dances and tunes appeared in altered forms in successive editions; some dropped out altogether after one or more appearances; while to every edition a varying number of new dances was added.

Of the earlier editions of this incomparable work John Playford was publisher, and, probably, editor as well. That he was not, however, the sole editor may, I think, be inferred from the different styles displayed in the wording of the notations. What precisely was the part which Playford and his assistants played in the compilation of the book, one can but conjecture.

It has already been pointed out (*see* Part I.) that the Country Dance ordinarily consisted of a series of figures arbitrarily chosen to fit a given tune, and that it was only rarely that any one of these became stereotyped by usage and achieved universal acceptance. The mere composition of the dances in "The Dancing Master" would, therefore, present no difficulty to one versed in the technique of the dance and acquainted with the ballad and instrumental airs of the day. We may, then, presume that the bulk of the book consists of dances so put together by Playford and his sub-editors, and the remainder of older dances that had, perhaps for many generations, been danced in the same way and to the same tunes.

Be this as it may, " The English Dancing Master " was the first collection of its kind published in this country; and, as it held the field unchallenged for upwards of half a century, it contains all that is now known respecting the forms and figures of the Country Dance in the latter half of the seventeenth century.

Now this was in fact a critical moment in the history of the Country Dance. It was a transitional period during which two important, though by no means unrelated, developments were in progress. In the first place, it coincided with the decline from popular favour of the older forms of the dance, the Rounds, Squares, Longs-for-four, six or eight performers, and the gradual evolution of that form which eventually superseded them, and was known as the " Longways for as many as will." This process may be traced in the successive editions of " The Dancing Master." In the first edition, for instance, out of 104 dances only 38, that is, a bare third, are Longways dances ; in the seventh edition, which represents chronologically the middle period of the publication, more than half—116 out of 208—are of this type ; while of the 918 dances contained in the three volumes of the seventeenth edition, all save 14 belong to the Longways species. I believe I am correct in saying that, except in the later editions of " The Dancing Master," one may search in vain the numerous Country Dance collections of the eighteenth century, published by Walsh, Pippard, Waylett, and others, for a single example of any one of the older forms of the dance. In this unique publication, then, we have our only source of information respecting the early and, what were probably, the original forms of the Country Dance.

During this same period, too, the Country Dance of the village green, the farmhouse, and the dancing booths of the annual fairs, was slowly invading the parlours and drawing-rooms of the wealthy, competing in attractiveness with the Minuets, Courantes, Gavottes, and rapidly gaining favour with the upper classes. It is, no doubt, true that the dance had never been the exclusive possession of any one class; but in the early days of its history, it was regarded by the educated less as a rival than an agreeable alternative, a refreshing contrast to the more formal and conventional dance of polite society. So long as the Country Dance was so regarded, it suffered little or no injury by transference from cottage to castle; but when, as time went on, it challenged, on its own merits, the supremacy of the drawing-room dances, the dance was at once subjected to an enervating influence which, paralysing its powers of resistance, ultimately led to its corruption. The decline was hastened when, as was inevitable, it attracted the notice, and fell into the hands of, the professional dancing master. He, *more suo*, sought to embroider upon it the fashionable steps of the day, to stifle it with the artificial graces and genteel posings of the drawing-room until, in a short time, of the freshness, spontaneity, and "gay simplicity" of the people's dance very little remained.

This development, moreover, seems to have synchronized with the displacement of the older forms of the dance. And this is quite intelligible. For the Rounds, Squares, etc., did not readily lend themselves to drawing-room treatment; and so long, therefore, as dances of this type only were exploited by the upper classes, there was no reason why the Country Dance should not retain unsullied its distinctive character. On the other hand, in the Longways dance the professor of dancing found a form easily adapted to the genteel style which he affected. Attracted, therefore, by this form alone, he forced it into prominence to the exclusion of the earlier and less flexible types.

The two movements cannot be dissociated. The increasing popularity of the Country Dance in the drawing-room led by a natural sequence to the rejection of the old-fashioned dances in favour of the more formal Longways dance. It is significant, too, that whenever the Country Dance is mentioned in early literature, or in connection with the Court functions of the sixteenth or seventeenth centuries, the reference is invariably to one or other of its older types. It is " Trenchmore " that Selden, for example, mentions as a favourite Court dance in the reign of Queen Elizabeth ; it is " Dargason " and " Sellenger's Round " that are mentioned in old books. There is, moreover, the well-known passage in Pepys's diary in which he describes a Court dance at which he was present on the last day of the year 1662. The diarist, it will be remembered, tells us that the first dance was the Brantle. " After that," he continues, " the King led a lady a single Coranto ; and then the rest of the lords, one after another, other ladies ; very noble it was, and great pleasure to see. Then to country dances ; the King leading the first, which he called for ; which was, says he, ' Cuckolds all awry,' the old dance of England." The " old dance of England " is, no doubt, identical with Playford's " Cuckolds all a row " ; it is included in every edition of " The Dancing Master," and, under its alternative title, " Hey, boys, up go we," is given in the text. It is a dance " for foure," that is, one of the old forms of the Country Dance, and is pretty certain to have been familiar to Pepys; for on Nov. 22nd, 1662, he records : " This day I bought the book of country dances against my wife's woman Gosnell comes, who dances finely; and there, meeting Mr. Playford, ..."

It was not, then, until the Longways dance had ousted the Rounds, Squares, etc., that the Country Dance became firmly established in the drawing-rooms and assembly halls. After that, its corruption followed as a matter of course, as we shall now see.

The first scientific, as opposed to popular, work on this subject was written by John Essex—" A Treatise on Chorography, or the art of dancing Country Dances " (1710). It contains an abridged version of Feuillet's chorography together with ten Country Dances technically described by means of that system. Now these dances differ very materially in character from those edited by Playford. They are one and all of the Longways type, set to derived tunes, and it is abundantly clear that they were intended to cater for the tastes of those who moved in polite circles.

The enervating tendency, exhibited here in a comparatively mild form, becomes much more strongly marked in Kellom Tomlinson's " Art of Dancing " (1735), wherein the author blandly apologises for mentioning the Country Dance in a work of which it was his original design " only to have spoke of genteel Dancing " ; yet, he continues, " as Country Dancing is become as it were the Darling or favourite Diversion of all Ranks of People from the Court to the Cottage in their different manners of Dancing, and as the Beauty of this agreeable Exercise (I mean when perform'd in the genteel Character) is very much eclipsed and destroyed by certain Faults, or Omissions, ... I shall, at the Request of some Persons of Figure, my Subscribers, endeavour to point out those Neglects which render this Diversion, to fine Dancers, either altogether disagreeable, or much less pleasant."

A few years later, 1752, Nicholas Dukes, who, like Tomlinson, was a professional dancing master, published " A Concise and easy method of Learning the Figuring Part of Country Dances," in which he takes " the liberty to acquaint every Gentleman or Lady who is desirous of performing Country Dances in a Genteel, free and easy manner, the necessity they are under of being first duly Qualified in a Minuet, that beautiful dance being so well calculated and adapted as to give room for every person to display all the Beauties and Graces of the body which becomes a genteel Carriage." It would, perhaps, be difficult to imagine anything more alien to the spirit of the Country Dance than the ultra-refined, exotic Minuet ; and that a man of authority in the dancing world should perceive an affinity between the two, shows the direction in which the evolution of the Country Dance was tending. It should be noticed, also, that the " men " and " women " of Playford have now become " gentlemen " and " ladies "—a very significant change.

It would be wearisome as well as profitless to follow, step by step, the successive stages through which the Country Dance passed in the course of its devolution. The process of corruption continued without break until the middle of the nineteenth century, soon after which time its popularity waned, and it was dethroned and superseded by the waltz, polka, etc.

I cannot, however, forbear mentioning Thomas Wilson, a very celebrated professor of dancing who, in the first quarter of the nineteenth century, published several books on the subject. His comments upon the earlier collections of Country Dances are very instructive. In one passage he satirises what he is pleased to call their "innovations on the true principles of English Country Dancing." The " true principles " are, of course, those which he expounds with such unction in his own books ; while the " innovations "— a curiously inapt word—refer to the figures described by Playford and his immediate successors which, he says, " were productive of the ridiculous antics and movements (afterwards particularised) and set to tunes equally absurd, both as to the style of the Music, and the length of the Strains." He adds that " the steps used in the old Country Dancing were equally absurd with the Figures," and " the effect they would have at Court, in these more enlightened times, may be better conceived than described," a remark for which I have no doubt there was plenty of justification.

Unhappily, the injurious effects of its excursion into the drawing-rooms of the upper classes, reacted, to some extent, upon the dance in the country villages ; and it needs no

Parfons Farewell

For four

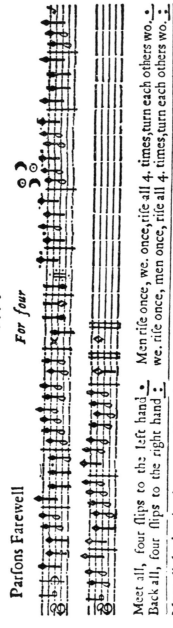

Meet all, four flips to the left hand ⦂
Back all, four flips to the right hand ⦂

Meet all, lead each others wo. a D. to the left hand ⦂ Change hands, meet again, take your own we. and to your places ⦂

Take your own with both hands, and meet with four flips, take the Co. we. four flips to the left hand ⦂ Meet again, take your own, and to your places ⦂

Men rife once, we. once, rife all 4. times, turn each others wo. ⦂
we. rife once, men once, rife all 4. times, turn each others wo. ⦂

Men meet, crofs right hands, then left pafs over, turn each others wo. with your right hand, crofs to your place again, and turn your own ⦂ We. as much with the Co. hands ⦂

Turn your own with your right hands, men crofs and go all the S. Hey to the Co. fide, and turn your own ⦂ Turn your own with the left hands, W⦂ crofs, go the S. Hey to your places, and turn your own ⦂

H 3

acute critic to detect this in the traditional Country Dance of the present day. The older forms of the dance have entirely disappeared, and the dances now extant belong exclusively to the Longways type.

These considerations materially enhance the value and interest attached to Playford's book, and we cannot be too thankful for the good fortune which has preserved a volume by means of which we can, if we will, reconstruct and revive the English Country Dance as it was danced in the days of its prime.

But to do this we must first master Playford's notations and translate them into modern and intelligible language. And this is no easy task. This book represents a modest attempt in this direction, made, however, not without a full appreciation of the difficulties involved in the undertaking and of the responsibility attaching to it.

In order that the reader may understand the nature of the problem, and estimate the value of the tentative solution here offered, I will now explain the scope of "The English Dancing Master," the character and the arrangement of its contents.

The first two pages of the book contain a list of the abbreviations used in the notations, together with the definitions of two movements (" The Single " and " The Double "), and of one figure (" Set and turn Single "). On each of the remaining pages of the book the tune and notation of a single dance are printed, with a diagram showing the positions of the performers at the beginning of the dance (*see* Plates facing pp. 13 and 72). The notation, which is printed immediately below the tune, is divided into Parts by horizontal lines drawn across the page. This division into Parts, all of which are of equal duration in performance, is made for the sake of clearness. The same device was employed by Essex, who likened the Parts to the "several verses of songs upon the same tune."

The Parts are further subdivided by vertical spaces into sections, each section containing the description of those

Country Dance Book.—Part II. B

movements and figures which are to be performed to the particular strain of the tune under which it is printed.

Now, it should be clearly understood that these notations deal with the figures and evolutions only. No instructions whatever are given there or elsewhere (with the single exception noted above) concerning the steps with which the figures are to be executed, the editor judging, no doubt correctly, that to the public he was addressing such directions would be superfluous. Playford's silence on this important branch of the subject opens up a very difficult question, which will presently engage our attention.

The next difficulty is to extract their meaning from the notations. These are couched in the colloquial speech of the day, with a sprinkling of technical terms, the whole resulting in a species of quasi-technical jargon not unlike that spoken by expert Morris and Country Dancers of the present day. The editor appears to have used the homely phrases that were current amongst dancers in his day; but these, intelligible enough to his contemporaries, often read to us as though they were written in a foreign tongue. Moreover, apart from their phraseology, the sentences are often ungrammatical, badly punctuated, involved, and ambiguous. Such a passage as the following—and it is a fair sample—looks at first sight as though it must for ever remain unintelligible :—"First man and 2 Wo. the 2 man and first Wo. lead out to the wall, and fall back again, while the other four crosse over each with his own, and meeting each other We. lead them under the first and 2 Cu. arms, falling into your places, and turn his own." Even when the meaning of the abbreviations are known, such a passage as this needs careful handling. Nevertheless, to give him his due, Playford is sometimes concise, lucid, and even racy. Such directions as "That again," "Women as much," "Do this to the last, the rest following and doing the like," are at once clear in their meaning and refreshing in their terseness.

In dealing with these notations a wide and detailed knowledge of the figures of the Morris, Sword, and Country dances of the present day, and also of the figures described in the dance manuals of the last two centuries, is essential. For the rest, all that can be done is patiently to study and analyse the sentences as one would do those of an unknown code, comparing, for instance, the several ways in which the same or similar expressions are used in different contexts, and so forth. On the whole I am inclined to believe that when these notations have attracted the general attention of students accustomed to work of this kind, it will be found quite possible to reconstruct the greater number, if not all of the dances. For my own part I have already deciphered, more or less to my own satisfaction, very nearly all the dances in the first four editions of " The Dancing Master," upon which I have as yet almost exclusively concentrated my attention ; and I am bold enough to believe that the notations of the thirty dances given in the text are substantially accurate.

The dances described by Playford are of seven species, viz., the Round; the Square for eight; the Long for four, six, or eight performers; the Longways for as many as will; and the dance for an indefinite number of couples standing in a straight line. Of the last variety " Dargason " is the sole example.

The Rounds, which are danced by three, four, or an indefinite number of couples, are the easiest of the Playford dances to interpret, although some of them—"Newcastle," for example—contain movements far from simple. Occasionally, a progressive figure of an elementary character appears in the Round, but such occurrences are rare. The first edition contains 14 examples of this type of dance ; the seventh edition, 25; and the last, 3 only. Five Rounds are noted in the text.

In the Square for eight we have the prototype of the French *conterdanse*, of which the Quadrille and Lancers still survive. In its construction and figures it is very similar to the Round for eight, as a comparison with "Newcastle " will show. Judging from the few examples of the Square that Playford gives, this particular form of Country Dance was never a very popular one. The first edition, for instance, contains 3 examples only; the seventh, 5; and the seventeenth, 2. Two examples, taken, respectively, from the first and third editions, are noted in the text.

The Longs-for-four are usually somewhat elaborate because, progressive movements being impracticable with so small a number of performers, the interest can only be maintained by a continuous series of varied figures. Some of the evolutions in these dances were afterwards utilised in the Longways dances, of which the Long-for-four formed the nucleus—the duple minor-set. Some of the dances, *e.g.*, " Cuckolds all a row " and " The Glory of the West," although arranged for four performers in the earlier editions, appear later on as dances for eight. Playford gives eight dances of this species in his first edition; nine in the seventh; and one example only in the last. Five varieties of varying difficulty are given in the text.

The Longs-for-six are especially interesting, in that they are cast in the same formation as that of the normal Morris dance. Many of the movements and figures are identical with those used in the latter dance, *e.g.*, Corners, Foot-up, Back-to-back, Hey for-three, etc. One figure, which occurs in " Grimstock," " Trenchmore," and other dances, is very similar to the well known sword dance figure " The Roll." A progressive movement, necessarily very simple and restrained, enters into a few of the dances of this type. For the rest, the Longs-for-six are easy of execution, pleasant to dance, and pretty to watch. These reasons may, perhaps, account for their popularity in the old days; for Playford gives no less than 25 examples in his first edition, and the same number in the seventh. Later on, however, their popularity seems to have decreased, for their number gradually lessened in the following issues, until in the final edition not a single example is printed. Four dances of this species are given in the text.

The Longs-for-eight, in construction and in the arrangement of their figures, are very similar to the Longs-for-six.

In some of the dances of both species the disposition of the dancers is irregular, an arrangement which often leads to some pretty and unusual combinations. Most of these abnormal forms, are, however, very difficult to decipher. For this reason I have been unable to give more than one example of this type, viz., "The Ten Pound Lass." There are eight dances of this class in the first edition; three in the seventh; and eight in the last. Three varieties are given in the text.

An especial interest attaches to the Longways dances in "The Dancing Master," for they represent the earliest examples of that type which, as we have seen, subsequently superseded all the others. In the seventeen editions we can trace, step by step, the gradual evolution of this type of dance, and especially of the progressive principle which eventually became its dominant feature.

We have already pointed out that in the older types of Country Dance progressive movements were only used very rarely and tentatively. This is also true of the majority of the Longways dances in the earlier editions. Some of these, *e.g.*, "Goddesses," contain no progressive movement whatever; in others it is introduced in one or other of the Parts only. In "Staines Morris," for example, every alternate Part is progressive, and in these progressive Parts two performers only participate, the first man and the last woman. The progressive movement is, moreover, confined to the woman's side only. Technically, the dance is a poor one, because in the progressive Parts, that is, for half the dance, two only of the performers have anything to do. To the student, however, the dance is full of interest, for in it he can see the progressive principle in embryo. "The Dancing Master" contains other dances of the same kind, but, as these are all more or less unattractive from the dancer's point of view, I have included this one example only.

In a few of the Longways dances the progressive movement leaves the dancers "improper," *i.e.*, with the man on the woman's side, and the woman on the man's. This produces a situation of complexity, which is explained—not, however, very lucidly—by Essex. The device, never frequently employed, gradually fell into disfavour and, finally, in the course of the eighteenth century, it disappeared altogether.

Nine Longways dances are given in the text. Of these, only one represents the dance in its full development, "The Twenty-ninth of May," and that has been taken from the seventh edition.

The figures which occur in the course of the dances described in "The Dancing Master" are very varied and very numerous. With the exception of the Set, the Side, the Honour, and others of a like character, all of which are essentially Country dance figures, I have been able to connect nearly all of them with similar evolutions in the Morris or Sword dances. The Whole-Poussette and, of course, the Roll, are sword-dance figures, and I believe that all those Country Dance figures, in which an arch is made by the joining of hands, handkerchiefs, or ribbons, were originally derived from the same source. Other evolutions such as Whole-Gip, Back-to-back, Cross-over, Foot-up, Corners, etc., are familiar Morris figures. The Hey, of course, is found in all three dances, in some form or other. This is at once the most engaging and the most varied and intricate of all the figures of the set-dance. There is an interesting passage in Hogarth's "Analysis of Beauty," in which he expatiates upon the beauty of this figure, which will perhaps bear quotation:—"The lines which a number of people together form in country or figure dancing, make a delightful play upon the eye, especially when the whole figure is to be seen at one view, as at the playhouse from a gallery ; the beauty of this kind of mystic dancing, as the poets term it, depends upon moving in a composed variety of lines, chiefly serpentine, governed by the principles of intricacy. The dances of barbarians are often represented without these movements, being only composed of wild skipping, jumping, and turning round, or running backward and forward, with convulsive shrugs and distorted gestures. One of the most pleasing movements in country dancing, and which answers to all the principles of varying at once, is what they call the hay. . . . . . There are other dances that entertain merely because they are composed of variety of movements and performed in proper time, but the less they consist of serpentine or waving lines, the lower they are in the estimation of dancing masters."

As already stated, Playford specifically defines two movements and one figure only. He describes the two movements, the Double and the Single, as, respectively, "four steps forward or backward closing both feet," and "two steps closing both feet"; and the figure, "Set and Turn Single," as "a Single to one hand, and a Single to the other and Turn Single."

This last expression, "Turn Single," is to be found upon almost every page of "The Dancing Master." The description of this movement in the text is founded upon that given by Nicholas Dukes in his "Country Dances" (1752), in which the figure is chorographically described. This removes all doubt as to the manner of its performance.

The rest of the figures described by Playford are, so far as the majority of them is concerned, fairly easy to interpret. Of those which occur in the dances given in the text, the only one about which I feel any doubt is the Side. "Sides all," "Arms as you Side," "First man Sides with first woman," are expressions which recur with great frequency. Although I have consulted all the sources of information at my disposal, I have been unable to find any authoritative definition of this figure. Nor have I been able to find any one of the above expressions, used in precisely the same way, in any of the dance collections subsequent to "The Dancing Master." I should have preferred to have omitted from the dances noted in this book all those in which this expression was used, but, owing to its frequent occurrence, this was quite impossible.

Some solution had, therefore, to be made. The one given in the text was arrived at by comparing the several ways in which

the term was used in various dances.   This made it clear
(1) that the figure was a four-bar movement; (2) that it was
executed by one dancer to another, or by two dancers, usually
partners, to each other simultaneously; (3) that it was a movement of courtesy similar to the Set; (4) and, lastly, that it
consisted of two movements of equal duration, half to
the right and half to the left.   This latter attribute, which
is a very important one, was deduced from " Nonesuch "
(*see* p. 116), where the figure in question is described as
" Side to the right " and " Side to the left," with a turn
Single added after each movement, thus converting the
movement into one of eight instead of four bars.

The most that can be said in favour of the solution I have
ventured to give, is that it fulfils all the above requirements;
and that it is difficult to think of any other movement which
will do so.   Nevertheless, I am aware that, although the
margin of doubt has been materially reduced, I have not
succeeded in eliminating it.

Before leaving the discussion of the figures it should be
explained that in the seventeenth century it was customary to
set several short figures to a single strain of the tune instead
of one or, at the most, two longer figures as afterwards
became the practice.   This, while it increased the difficulty of
the dance, made the use of elaborate steps impracticable.   It
added, however, to the brightness and briskness of the
dance, and it is in this respect, no doubt, that the seventeenth century Country Dance differs most from that of
later days.

Upon the subject of the steps, as I have already pointed out,
Playford is silent.   Hence the steps described in this book,
are not, like the figures and music, authoritative; they are
merely those which my researches lead me to believe were
actually, or at any rate, very probably, used in the
seventeenth century Country Dance.   I have arrived at this
somewhat speculative solution of a very difficult question,
(1) by observing the steps used in the traditional Country

Dance of the present day ; and (2) by examining the evidence bearing upon the subject, contained in the dance manuals of the last two centuries.

All the five steps described in the text are still used by traditional dancers ; other steps are also used, *e.g.*, polka, galop, and waltz steps ; but these I rejected, because, like the figures with which they are nearly always associated, they are obviously of more modern derivation.

Nearly all the dance books subsequent to " The Dancing Master " contain directions concerning the steps to be used in country dancing. In most cases, however, the steps recommended are those of the Gavotte, Bourrée, Minuet, Rigadoon, and similar dances ; but these were the product of a later development, and are not what we are looking for, Fortunately, information of another and more helpful kind may occasionally be gleaned from the books of the more sagacious writers.

Essex, for instance, tells us that " the most ordinary steps in Country Dances (except those that are upon Minuet airs) are steps of Gavot, drive sideways, Bourrée step and some small jumps forward of either foot in a hopping manner, or little hopps in all round figures . . . . . One may make little hopps or Bourrée steps but little hopps are more in fashion . . . . . In all figures that go forwards, or backwards and forwards, always make gavotte steps. In all figures that go sideways drive sideways."

Now, the " drive sideways " is the same as the " slip " (*see* p. 37) ; " the small jumps forward of either foot in a hopping manner," I take to be the " skipping step " (*see* p. 36), while the "little hopps in all round figures " is obviously " the double-hop " (*see* p. 38). So that for three of my five steps I can claim the authority of a scientific writer, who lived and wrote during the actual publication of " The Dancing Master." For the two remaining steps—the " walking " and " running " steps—traditional authority is so strong that I do not think that any reasonable doubt can be raised with respect to their authenticity.

Essex, it is true, also mentions Gavotte, Bourrée, and Rigadoon steps; but these, I think, we must ignore. In recommending them he was following or, maybe, initiating a fashion which, as we know, subsequently led to the degeneracy of the Country Dance. Moreover, when offering the alternative of Bourrée steps or "little hopps," Essex admitted that the latter were "more in fashion."

As time went on, the practice of substituting the mo:e ornate steps of the Court Dance for those of the Country Dance gradually became universal. Nevertheless, here and there, writers are to be found who warned their readers against this prevailing and undesirable habit. Indeed, as late as 1818, we find a protest of this nature in Barclay Dun's " Translation of nine of the most fashionable quadrilles . . . to which are prefixed a few observations on the style, etc., of the Quadrille, the English Country Dance, and the Scotch Reel." In this most interesting work, the author quotes with approbation from " a small volume said to be written by a lady of distinction," to the following effect :—" The characteristic of our English country-dance is that of gay simplicity. The steps should be few and easy, and the corresponding motion of the arms and body unaffected, modest, and graceful."

To these wise words Dun himself adds the following comments :—" As it is the province of the dance to imitate most scrupulously the accent or expression of the music, and as the English tunes are well known to possess less variety of expression and modulation than those of France, I would recommend the use of the most simple and neatly constructed steps in this kind of dancing ; practice will enable the dancer to perform them in that correct, light, and prompt manner which the nature of the music requires."

It would, I think, be difficult to offer the would-be performer of Playford's dances wiser or more salutary advice than that given by the " lady of distinction." The dominant characteristic of our traditional Country Dance is, undoubtedly, its

" gay simplicity " ; and it is precisely because drawing-room steps and mannerisms conflict with this, that they must be ruled out as wholly unsuitable.

We see, then, that although in the nature of things it is impossible to speak dogmatically with regard to the steps which should or should not be used in the Playford dances, it is quite feasible to suggest those which are in harmony with their natural and simple character, and for which at least some semblance of authority can fairly be claimed.

I would add that there is, of course, no authority whatever for the particular steps that are attached to the figures in the notations—I mean, so far as their distribution is concerned. They merely represent the steps which appear to me to be the most suitable, taking into consideration the character of each figure and of the dance in which it occurs. This, however, is a matter of minor importance ; and dancers are, of course, at liberty to vary them as they please. I would, however, deprecate the introduction of steps other than those described in the text, unless supported by some equally trustworthy authority.

Our aim in reviving these dances should be to keep them fresh and natural and, to this end, to avoid the use of elaborate steps, together with the tricks and mannerisms of the theatre or of the drawing-room ; for that way, as history shows, danger lies. The steps that I have ventured to suggest may or may not be historically accurate ; but they can, at least, be executed without injury either to the form or spirit of our very beautiful national dance.

I cannot bring this Introduction to a close without saying something about the music. Upon comparing the same tunes in successive editions of " The Dancing Master," it will be found that many were subjected to frequent alteration. Remembering the standpoint from which the professional musician of those days regarded the music of the people, it is not difficult to conjecture the nature and purpose of these changes. Their object, of course, was to bring the tunes into conformity with the musical notions of the day. Indeed, I suspect that many of the "grosse errors" of the first edition were no more than modal peculiarities, which, by the suppression or addition of sundry accidentals, were subsequently "corrected" in the second and later editions. The wonder is, not so much that changes of this nature were made, as that the tunes were ever printed in the unedited forms in which many of them appear in the earlier editions. "Jenny Pluck Pears," for instance, appears as a dorian air in the first edition, thus:—

In the second edition, the dorian was converted into the minor mode:—

Finally, in the fourth and subsequent editions, by omitting the signature while retaining the added accidentals, the tune became a major one, and in the seventh edition took the following form:—

In the course of my investigations I have been much struck by the remarkable number of beautiful and characteristically English folk-airs that lie buried in "The Dancing Master." I am satisfied that the larger number of these are quite unknown to the average musician. Even among the few tunes which I have selected for the purpose of this volume, there are several fine and distinctive airs, *e.g.*, "Jenny Pluck Pears," "New Bo-Peep," "Ten Pound Lass," "Oranges and Lemons," "The Black Nag," "Rufty Tufty," "Saint Martin's," "Grimstock," "Putney Ferry," "Black Jack," etc., not one of which, so far as I know, has hitherto been published in an accessible form.

The fact is, that the only tunes in "The Dancing Master" at all widely known are those which first appeared in Chappell's "Popular Music of the Olden Time"; and many of these were unfortunately presented in anything but their best forms. For Chappell—as was, perhaps, natural, remembering the time at which he wrote—very often chose the later and "edited" forms in preference to the earlier and uncorrupted modal ones. This error of judgment has since been corrected by

Mr. Wooldridge in the second edition of "Popular Music." Moreover, the tunes which Chappell selected were chosen quite as much for their historical, literary, or antiquarian associations, as for their æsthetic and artistic qualities. Consequently, a large number of the best and most characteristic of the Playford tunes were omitted from Chappell's book; and of those included many, *e.g.*, "The Friar in the Well," "Staines Morris," "Nonesuch," etc., were first presented, and have since become popular, in more or less degenerate forms.

Again, it should be understood that the tunes in "The Dancing Master," are dance-airs, arranged for the "treble violin." They are instrumental, not vocal tunes. Originally, no doubt, they were ballad airs—their titles show this—but, as printed by Playford, they are derived tunes transformed under the influence of the dance, and of the instrument upon which they have been played. A few, *e.g.*, "Gathering Peascods" and "The Beggar Boy," are apparently vocal airs, pure and simple, which I suspect had not, before Playford so utilised them, been pressed into the service of the dance.

Be this as it may, by far the larger number of the tunes in "The Dancing Master" are genuine instrumental dance-tunes, whatever they may have been originally. To present these as vocal airs wedded to words is to disguise their true nature and beauty, and to deprive them of the appreciation otherwise their due.

In selecting the dances for the purpose of this volume, I have been guided by several and, in some cases, conflicting considerations. My choice was necessarily restricted (1) to those dances, the notations of which I was able to interpret satisfactorily; and (2) to those that from the dancer's point of view were most characteristic and interesting. Naturally, I found that many of the best tunes were attached to dances which for one or other of these reasons had to be excluded; while, *per contra*, dances otherwise free from objection were often allied to poor tunes. My selection had, therefore, to be a compromise. I might, of course, have transferred the good tunes mated to indifferent dances, to the good dances set to bad tunes. And remembering the arbitrary way in which Country Dances were often compounded, I should have had ample justification for adopting such a course. On reflection, however, I decided, so far as this book was concerned, to print for each dance the tune with which it is associated in "The Dancing Master." In future I may, perhaps, act differently.

The investigations which I have made in connection with this book have convinced me that in Playford's "Dancing Master" we possess a veritable treasure-house of precious material, the full value of which has yet to win general recognition. For those interested in the revival of folk-dancing, it is the only book in which the English Country Dance, in its earliest, purest, and most characteristic forms, is described. Furthermore, "The Dancing Master" contains the largest and, in some respects, the most authoritative collection of seventeenth century instrumental folk-tunes that we possess. For these two reasons alone—and others might easily be adduced—it is to be hoped that this unique work will some day attract from students of dancing, and from those interested in the folk-music of their country, the attention which it undoubtedly deserves but has not yet, I think, received.

THE DANCE.

THE ROOM.

THE following diagram is a ground plan of the room in which the dances are supposed to take place :—

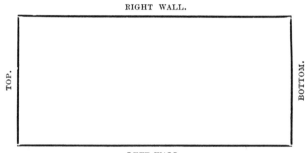

RIGHT WALL.

TOP.　　　　　　　　　　　　　　BOTTOM.

LEFT WALL.

A diagram, showing the initial disposition of the dancers, is printed at the head of the notation of each dance, and placed so that its four sides correspond with the four sides of the room as depicted in the above plan. That is, the upper and lower sides of the diagram represent, respectively, the right and left walls of the room; its left and right sides the top and bottom.

In Playford's time, the top of the room was called *the Presence*, alluding to the dais upon which the spectators were seated. The expression *facing the Presence* means, therefore, facing up, *i.e.*, toward the top of the room; while *back to the Presence* means facing down, toward the bottom of the room.

TECHNICAL TERMS AND SYMBOLS.

O = man ; ☐ = woman.

r. = a step taken with the right foot : **l.** = a step taken with the left foot.

h.r. = a hop on to the right foot ; **l.r.** = a hop on to the left foot.

The *Set* or the *General Set* is the area occupied or enclosed by the dancers in any given dance-formation.

A *Longways dance* is one in which the performers take partners and stand in two parallel lines, the men on one side opposite and facing their partners on the other, those on the men's side facing the right wall, those on the women's side the left wall.

The disposition of the dancers in a longways dance is said to be *proper* when the men and women are on their own sides; and *improper* when the men are on the women's side or the women on the men's.

A *Progressive dance* consists of the repetition for an indefinite number of times of a series of movements, called the *Complete Figure*, each repetition being performed by the dancers in changed positions. The performance of each Complete Figure is called a *Round*.

A *Progressive movement* or *figure* is one the performance of which leaves the dancers relatively in different positions.

A *neutral* dancer is one who, in a progressive dance, is passive during the performance of a Round.

In dances or figures in which two couples only are engaged, the terms *contrary woman* and *contrary man* are used to denote the woman or man other than the partner.

When two dancers standing side by side are directed to *take hands* they are to join inside hands : that is, the right hand of one with the left hand of the other, if the two face the same way ; and right hands or left hands, if they face in opposite directions. When they are directed to take, or give, right or left hands, they are to join right with right, or left with left.

To *cross hands* the man takes the right and left hands of the woman with his right and left hands respectively, the right hands being held above the left.

When two dancers face one another and are directed to take *both hands*, they are to join right with left and left with right.

To pass *by the right* is to pass right shoulder to right shoulder; *by the left*, left shoulder to left shoulder.

When two dancers pass each other they should always, unless otherwise directed, pass each other by the right.

When a woman's path crosses that of a man's, the man should allow the woman to pass first and in front of him.

When one dancer is directed to *lead* another, the two join right or left hands according as the second dancer stands on the right or left hand of the leader.

To *cast off* is to turn outward and dance outside the General Set.

To *cast up* or *cast down* is to turn outward and move up or down outside the General Set.

To *fall* is to dance backwards; to *lead*, or *move*, is to dance forwards.

To make a *half-turn* is to turn through half a circle and face in the opposite direction; to make a *whole-turn* is to make a complete revolution.

The terms *clockwise* and *counter-clockwise* are self-explanatory and refer to the direction of circular movements.

PROGRESSIVE DANCES.

THE PROGRESSIVE LONGWAYS DANCE.

There are two methods of progression in a Longways Dance —the *whole-set* and the *minor-set*.

In the *whole set* dance the progression is effected by the transference in every Round of the top couple from the top to the bottom of the General Set, the rest of the couples moving up one place.

The *minor-set* dance is one in which the Complete Figure in each Round is performed simultaneously by subsidiary sets or groups of two (*duple*) or three (*triple*) adjacent couples.

The effect of every performance of the Complete Figure is to change the positions of the couples in each minor-set. In a duple minor-set dance the two couples change places, in a triple minor-set the two upper couples. This necessitates a rearrangement of the minor-sets in the following Round, and this is effected by each top couple forming a new minor-set with the adjacent couple or couples below. In this way the top couple of each minor-set will move down the Set one place every Round; while the lower couple of the duple minor-set, and the second couple in the triple minor-set, will each move up one place. The position of the third couple in the triple minor-set will be unaffected, but in the following Round it will, as second couple, move up one place. As the dance proceeds, therefore, every couple will move from one end of the Set to the other, the top couples down, the rest up. In a duple minor-set dance each couple on reaching either end of the General Set becomes neutral in the following Round. In a triple minor-set each couple upon reaching the top of the General Set remains neutral during the two following Rounds; and on reaching the bottom for one Round only. It should be added that when the top couple of a triple minor-set dance reaches the last place but one it must, in the succeeding Round, dance the progressive portion of the Complete Figure with the last couple or change places with them.*

---

* For further and more detailed information respecting the Progressive Longways Dance see *The Country Dance Book.*

THE MUSIC.

The several strains of each dance-air will be marked in the music-book and in the notations by means of capital letters, A, B, C, etc. When a strain is played more than once in a Part it will be marked A1, B1, C1, etc., on its first performance, and A2, B2, C2, A3, B3, etc., in subsequent repetitions.

It will be found that many of the dances in this collection are divided into two or more Parts. John Essex quaintly but aptly likened these divisions to "the several verses of songs upon the same tune."

In non-progressive dances, the division is made merely for the sake of clearness in description; the Parts are intended to follow on without pause.

When, however, a progressive movement occurs in one or other of the figures of a Part, that Part must be repeated as often as the dancers decree. The usual practice is to repeat the Part until the leader has returned to his original place.

Progressive figures will be marked as such in the notation; while the Parts in which they occur will be headed "Whole-Set," "Duple Minor-Set," etc., according to the nature of the progression.

MOTION IN THE DANCE.

The Country Dance is pre-eminently a figure dance, depending in the main for its expressiveness upon the weaving of patterned, concerted evolutions rather than upon intricate steps or elaborate body-movements. That the steps in the Country Dance should be few in number and technically simple is, therefore, natural enough. For complicated foot-work is obviously incompatible with that free, easy, yet controlled, movement needed in the execution of intricate figures. In a figure-dance such as we are now considering, the way in which the dancer moves from place to place is obviously of far greater importance than the steps, and to this therefore we will first turn our attention. An analysis of the way in which the traditional folk-dancer moves shows that it is based upon two main principles :—

(1.) The weight of the body in motion must always be supported wholly on one foot or the other, and never carried on both feet at the same moment. From this it follows that the transition from step to step, *i.e.*, the transference of the weight from one foot to the other, must always be effected by spring, high enough to raise the body off the ground.

(2.) The motive force, although derived in part from this foot-spring, is chiefly due to the action of gravity, brought into play by the inclination of the body from the vertical. The dancer in motion is always in unstable equilibrium, regulating both the speed and the direction of his movement by varying the poise and balance of his body. When moving along the straight, for instance, his body will be poised either in front of his feet or behind them, according as his movement is forward or backward ; and laterally when moving along a curved track.

The function of the legs is to support the body rather than to help to move it forward, the actual motion being set up, regulated, and directed by the sway and balance of the body, as in skating. The body, it should be pointed out, cannot be used in this way, that is to set up and regulate motion, unless it is carried essentially in line from head to foot, without bend at the neck or at the waist, or sag at the knees.

The advantages of this way of moving are obvious. Motion is started and kept up with the least expenditure of muscular energy; it can be regulated, both as to speed and direction, with the greatest ease and nicety; above all, its expressive value is high in that it brings the whole body, and not the legs alone, into play. This last consideration is a weighty one. The strongest argument against "leg-dancing" is not merely that it is ugly, or that it involves superfluous muscular effort, but that the legs, being primarily concerned and almost wholly occupied in supporting and preserving the equilibrium of the body, cannot effectively be employed for expressive or any other purpose.

THE STEPS.

The following general directions apply to the execution of all the steps used in the Country Dance :—

(1.) Country Dance steps always fall on the main divisions of the bar, *i.e.*, on each of the two beats in duple measure ($\frac{2}{2}$ or $\frac{6}{8}$), and of the three beats in triple-measure ($\frac{3}{2}$ or $\frac{9}{8}$). In the case of a compound step, that is, one that comprises more than one movement, the accented movement should fall on the beat.

(2.) The step should fall on the ball of the foot, not on the toe, with the heel off, but close to, the ground.

(3.) The feet should be held straight and parallel, neither turned out nor in at the ankle.

(4.) The legs should never be straddled, but held close together. Nor again should they be extended more than is absolutely necessary; the spring should as far as possible take the place of the stride.

(5.) The jar caused by the impact of the feet on the floor should be absorbed mainly by the ankle-joint, and very little or not at all by the knees. The knee should be bent as little as possible, so little that the supporting leg should appear to be straight, *i.e.*, in one line from hip to ankle.

(6.) All unnecessary movements should be suppressed, *e.g.*, kicking up the heels, fussing with the feet, raising the knees, etc.

THE RUNNING-STEP.

This is the normal Country Dance step. It is an ordinary running-step, executed neatly and lightly, in accordance with the above instructions.

In the notation this will be marked :—

r.s. (running-step).

THE WALKING-STEP.

This is a modified form of the running-step, in which the spring, though present, is scarcely noticeable.

In the notation this will be marked :—

w.s. (walking-step).

SKIPPING-STEP.

This is the usual step-and-hop on alternate feet. The accent is on the step, which must fall, therefore, on the beat. Care should be taken to prevent the skipping-step from degenerating into a double-hop, the two feet taking the ground together, instead of in succession. The hop should fall on the last quarter, or the last third, of the beat according as the latter is simple or compound, thus :—

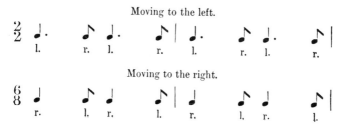

In the notation this will be marked :—

sk.s. (skipping-step).

SLIPPING-STEP.

This is a series of springs, made sideways, off alternate feet, the major spring being on to the outside foot, *i.e.*, the left when going to the left and the right when going to the right. Although the legs are thus alternately opening and closing, scissor-fashion, the motion is effected almost wholly by the spring, not the straddle ; the legs, therefore, should be separated as little as possible. The free foot should not be allowed to scrape the ground.

The accent falls on the foot on to which the major spring is made, that is, the left or right, according to the direction of motion, thus :—

In the notation this will be marked :—

sl.s. (slipping-step).

THE DOUBLE-HOP.

This is sometimes, though very rarely, used in ring movements as an alternative to the slipping-step. It is a variant of the Slip, in which the feet, instead of taking the ground separately one after the other, alight together a few inches apart.

THE SINGLE.

Playford defines the Single as " two steps, closing the feet." Technically this may be interpreted in the following way : on the first beat of the bar a spring is made, forwards or sideways, on to one foot, say the right ; the left foot is then brought up beside it, the weight wholly or in part momentarily supported upon it, and, on the second beat of the bar, transferred to the right foot in position.

This step is subject to various modifications, partly individual, but more often arising from the character of the dance or phrase in which the step occurs. Many dancers, for instance, never allow the foot upon which the initial spring is made (*i.e.*, the right foot in the above description) to leave the ground when the left foot is brought up beside it ; but instead, rise on the toes of both feet on the intermediate accent, and then on the second beat sink back on to the ball of the right foot.

THE DOUBLE.

This is defined in *The English Dancing Master* as " four steps forward or backward closing the feet," *i.e.*, four running or walking steps, the last of which is made in position (that is, beside the other foot), the weight being supported either on the one foot or on both feet, according to circumstances.

THE TURN SINGLE.

The dancer makes a whole turn on his axis, clockwise (unless otherwise directed), taking four (in triple measure, three or six) low springing steps off alternate feet, beginning with the right foot. The body must be held erect, and the turn regulated so that the dancer completes the circle and regains his original position on the last step.

In the notations specific steps are in some cases prescribed, but these are not to be regarded as obligatory. When no directions are given the choice of step must be determined by the performers themselves. In such cases dancers should remember (1) that the running-step is the normal Country Dance step, and that it is only in comparatively few cases that any other step can be effectively substituted for it ; (2) that slipping and skipping steps, being compound steps, occupy more time in their execution than the " simple " running-step, and should not therefore be used except in dances of slow or moderate time ; (3) that it is not necessary for every dancer to use the same step at the same time ; nor, again, is it necessary (4) that a single figure should always be danced to one step throughout—the arbitrary change of step in the course of a movement is not only permissible, but is in many cases to be commended.

ARMS AND HANDS.

Nearly all the prescribed arm-movements in the Country Dance relate to the joining of hands. Of ornamental or fanciful movements there are none, nor any of formal design that are devised—like many of the arm-movements of the Morris Dance—to assist the actions of the dancer. Nevertheless, perhaps for this reason, the carriage and manipulation of the hands and arms form a very characteristic feature of the Country Dance.

It may be taken as a general rule that when the arms are not in active use, *i.e.*, when they are not being directly employed for some specific purpose, they should be allowed to swing quietly and loosely by the side. This involves complete relaxation of the muscles that control the shoulder, elbow, and wrist joints, and the capacity to resist sympathetic, involuntary tension in other muscles.

The dancer may sometimes find it necessary to make use of his arms to maintain his balance, *e.g.*, to throw out the outside arm when moving swiftly round a sharp curve. This is permissible, provided that such movements are made only when really necessary, simply, and without exaggeration.

All the prescribed hand and arm movements in the Country Dance have a definite purpose, and in their execution no more is required of the dancer than that he should fulfil this purpose effectively and in the simplest and most direct way. For instance, in " leading " the taking of hands is not a mere formality ; the dancer should actually lead—that is, support his partner, guide and regulate her movement.

THE JOINING OF HANDS.

In linking right hand with right, or left with left, the hands are held sideways (*i.e.*, in a vertical plane), thumbs uppermost, and brought lightly together, not clenched, the four fingers of each hand resting on the palm of the other, and the thumb pressing on the knuckle of the middle finger. The hands should be joined in this manner in leading, in handing in the Hey, and in the Turn-with-one-hand.

In joining inside hands, that is, right hand with left, or left hand with right, *e.g.*, in rings, the Turn, the Poussette, etc., the man holds his hand palm upward, the woman places her hand in his, and the fingers are clasped as before.

When two men or two women join inside hands, it is suggested that the dancer having the lower number should always take the man's position (*i.e.*, give his hand palm upward).

MOVEMENTS OF COURTESY.

THE HONOUR.

This is a formal obeisance made by partners to one another at the conclusion, and sometimes in the course, of the dance. The man bows, head erect, making a slight forward inclination of the body from the hips; the woman, placing her left foot behind the right, makes a quick downward and upward movement by bending and straightening the knees.

The honour should always be made in rhythm with the music and, if possible, in conjunction with some corresponding movement of the feet. The exact way in which this is done depends upon circumstances. The usual method is to place the right foot on the ground twelve inches or so to the side say, on the first beat of the bar, and to bring up the left foot beside it—or, in the case of the woman, behind it—on the following beat when the obeisance is made.

THE SET.

This is a movement of courtesy, addressed by one dancer to another, or more frequently by two dancers to each other simultaneously. It consists of a single to the right sideways, followed by a single to the left back to position (two bars).

THE SET-AND-HONOUR.

This is a lengthened form of the Set occupying four instead of two bars. On the first beat of the first bar the right foot is placed on the ground sideways to the right; on the first beat of the second bar the left foot is brought up beside it and the honour paid in the manner already explained (two bars). These movements are then repeated in the reverse direction, the left foot being moved to the side, the right foot brought up beside it, and the honour paid (two bars, *i.e.*, four bars in all).

THE SIDE.

This is performed by two dancers, usually partners, but not necessarily so. They face each other, and move forward a double obliquely to the right, *i.e.*, passing by the left. On the third step they make a half-turn counter-clockwise, completing the turn on the fourth step as they face one another (two bars). This completes the first half of the movement, and is called *side to the right*. In the second half of the movement, *side to the left*, the dancers retrace their steps along the same tracks, moving obliquely to the left (passing by the right), turn clockwise, and face each other on the fourth step. The whole movement occupies four bars of the music.

The dancers must remember to face each other at the beginning and close of each movement, to pass close to each other, shoulder to shoulder, and always to face in the direction in which they are moving.

ARM WITH THE RIGHT (OR LEFT).

Two performers, usually partners, meet, link right (or left) arms, swing round a complete circle, clockwise (or counter-clockwise) (two bars), separate, and fall back to places (r.s.) (two bars, *i.e.*, four bars in all).

In order that the dancers may give and receive mutual support in the execution of the whole turn, the arms, crooked at right angles, must be linked at the elbows, the dancers leaning slightly away from each other, so as to throw part of their weight on their arms.

THE FIGURES.

Figure 1.

HANDS-THREE, HANDS-FOUR, ETC.

Three or more dancers, as directed, form a ring, extend arms, join hands a little above waist-level, and dance round. In the absence of specific instructions to the contrary it is to be understood that one complete circuit is to be danced, clockwise, the performers facing centre.

The dancers should clasp hands firmly, lean outward, and thus support each other. When the movement is followed by a repetition in the reverse direction, counter-clockwise, the dancers may stamp on the first step of the second movement.

Occasionally this figure is performed with backs to the centre, the dancers facing outward.

When space is restricted and the ring reduced in size, and it is no longer feasible to extend the arms, the arms should be raised, sharply bent at the elbows (upper arms horizontal, fore-arms approximately vertical) and the hands joined above head-level. This, too, will be found to be the easier and more convenient method when the movement is slow and formal in character, as is not infrequently the case in back-rings (*e.g.*, the back-ring in " Fye, Nay, Prithee John," p. 122 Part VI).

Figure 2.

THE TURN.

Two dancers face one another, join both hands, swing once round clockwise (unless otherwise directed), separate, and fall back to places.

In turning, performers should clasp hands firmly, arms at full stretch, and lean back so as mutually to give and receive support. If either the skipping-step or running-step be used, the feet should be slightly crossed so that the dancers may face each other squarely throughout the movement.

FIGURE 3.
THE SWING.

This is similar to the preceding movement, the dancers however turning continuously and, on occasion, moving from place to place as directed.

FIGURE 4.
THE TURN WITH RIGHT OR LEFT HAND.

Two dancers join right or left hands, as directed, and move round a complete circle, separate, and fall back to places.

The carriage of the dancers and the position of their arms will depend upon the size of the circle described and the speed with which the figure is executed.   When eight steps are allotted to the figure the dancers should describe a large circle, lean slightly towards each other, and join hands above head-level. As the taking of hands in this case is for the purpose of balance rather than support, there is no pull on the arms and no necessity, therefore, to extend them at full stretch. The arms should, accordingly, be held loosely and slightly curved at the elbow (not bent at an angle).   If, however, the Turn has to be completed in four steps, the arms should be fully extended and the hands joined a little above waist-level, the dancers leaning away from and supporting each other ; while in still faster turns, where the dancers are compelled to turn in a very small circle (as in the Do-Si in the Running Set) they should join hands below waist-level with arms tense and sharply crooked at the elbow.

FIGURE 5.
RIGHT- (OR LEFT-) HANDS-ACROSS.

This is performed usually by four dancers (say, the first and second couples in a longways dance), but occasionally by three or six.

In the first case, first man and second woman join right (or left) hands, while second man and first woman do the same. Holding their hands close together, head-level, the four dancers dance round clockwise (or counter-clockwise), inclining inwards towards the centre, and facing in the direction they are moving.

When three performers only are engaged, two of them join hands and the third places his hand on theirs.

It is to be understood that the dancers make one complete circuit unless specific instructions to the contrary are given.

FIGURE 6.

HALF-POUSSETTE.

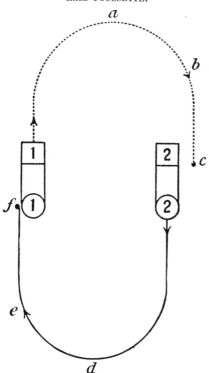

This is performed by two adjacent couples.

Each man faces his partner and takes her by both hands. The arms must be held out straight, and very nearly shoulder high.

Country Dance Book.—Part II.—D

First man, pushing his partner before him, moves four steps along dotted line to *a*, and then falls back four steps along the line *a b c* into the second couple's place, pulling his partner after him.

Simultaneously, second man, pulling his partner with him, falls back four steps along unbroken line to *d*, and then moves forward four steps along the line *d e f* into the first couple's place (four bars).

The above movement is called the half-poussette, and is, of course, a progressive figure.

When the half-poussette is followed by a repetition of the same movement, each couple describing a complete circle or ellipse, the figure is called the whole-poussette.

FIGURE 7.

BACK-TO-BACK.

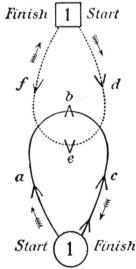

First man and first woman face each other and move forward, the man along the line *a b*, the woman along the dotted line *d e.* They pass by the right, move round each other, back to back, and fall back to places, the man along the line *b c,* the woman along the dotted line *e f.*

The arrow heads in the diagram show the positions of the dancers at the end of each bar, and point in the directions in which they are facing. The arrows alongside the lines show the direction in which the dancers move.

FIGURE 8.

WHOLE-GIP FACING CENTRE.

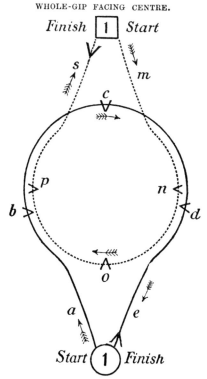

Finish | 1 | *Start*

s

m

c

p

n

b

d

o

a

e

Start (1) *Finish*

First man moves forward along line *a,* dances round circle *b c d,* facing the centre, and falls back along line *d e* to place;

while first woman dances along dotted line *m*, moves round circle *n o p*, facing the centre, and falls back along dotted line *p s* to place (four bars). In the execution of the running-step the feet will have to be slightly crossed in order that the dancers may face each other squarely throughout the movement.

The arrows and arrow heads have the same signification as in the preceding figure.

FIGURE 9.

WHOLE-GIP FACING OUTWARD.

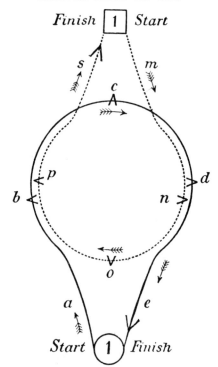

First man moves along line *a* and dances round circle *b c d*, facing outward to place; while first woman moves along dotted line *m*, dances round circle *n o p*, facing outward, and moves along dotted line *p s* to place (four bars).

––––––––

THE HEY.

The Hey may be defined as the rhythmical interlacing in serpentine fashion of two groups of dancers, moving in single file and in opposite directions.

The figure assumes different forms according to the disposition of the dancers. These varieties, however, fall naturally into two main types according as the track described by the dancers—disregarding the deviations made by them in passing one another—is (1) a straight line, or (2) the perimeter of a closed figure, circle, or ellipse.

The second of these species, as the simpler of the two, will be first explained.

Figure 10.

THE CIRCULAR HEY.

In the analysis that follows the circle will, for the sake of convenience, be used throughout to represent the track described by the dancers in this form of the figure. In the round dance the track will of course be a true circle; while in the square dance it will become one as soon as the move-

ment has begun.   On the other hand, in a longways dance,
the formation will be elliptical rather than circular, but this
will not affect the validity of the following explanation.

In the circular-hey the dancers, who must be even in
number, are stationed at equal distances around the circum-
ference of a circle, facing alternately in opposite directions,
thus :—

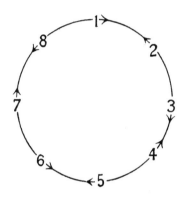

Diagram 4.

Odd numbers face and move round clockwise ;   even
numbers counter-clockwise.   All move at the same rate and,
upon meeting, pass alternately by the right and left.

This progression is shown in diagram 5, the dotted and
unbroken lines indicating the tracks described respectively
by odd and even numbers.   It will be seen that in every
circuit the two opposing groups of dancers, odd and even,
thread through each other twice ; that is, there will be eight

simultaneous passings, or *changes*, as we will call them, in each complete circuit :—

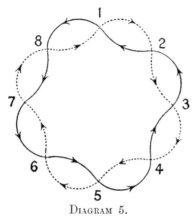

DIAGRAM 5.

This movement is identical with that of the Grand Chain, except that in the familiar Lancers figure the performers take hands, alternately right and left, as they pass; whereas, in the Country Dance hey, "handing," as Playford calls it, is the exception rather than the rule.

In this form the hey presents no difficulty. No misconception can arise so long as (1) the initial dispositions of the pairs, and (2) the duration of the movement, measured by circuits or changes, are clearly defined ; and instructions on these two points will always be given in the notation. It should be understood that in the absence of directions to the contrary (1) the first pass is by the right, and (2) the dancers pass without handing.

FIGURE 11.

PROGRESSIVE CIRCULAR HEY.

Sometimes the hey is danced progressively, the dancers beginning and ending the movement pair by pair, instead of simultaneously, as above described. This is effected in the following way :—

The first change is performed by one pair only, say Nos. 1 and 2 (see diagram 4, Fig. 10); the second by two pairs, Nos. 1 and 3, and Nos. 2 and 8; the third in like manner by three pairs, and the fourth by four pairs. At the conclusion of the fourth change Nos. 1 and 2 will be face to face, each having traversed half a circuit, and all the dancers will be actively engaged, thus:—

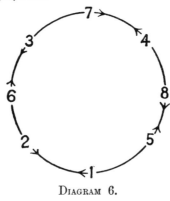

DIAGRAM 6.

The movement now proceeds in the usual way. At the end of every complete circuit the position will be as follows:—

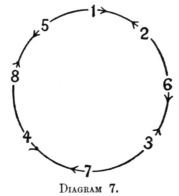

DIAGRAM 7.

The figure is concluded in the following manner :—
Nos. 1 and 2, upon reaching their original places (see
diagram 7), stop and remain neutral for the rest of the
movement. The others continue dancing until they reach
their proper places, when they, in like manner, stop and
become neutral. This they will do, pair by pair, in the
following order, Nos. 3 and 8, 4 and 7, 5 and 6. The initial
and final movements thus occupy the same time, *i.e.*, four
changes.

Whenever the progressive hey occurs (1) the initial pair
will be named ; and (2) the duration of the movement,
measured by changes or circuits, will be given in the notation.

Figure 12.

THE STRAIGHT HEY.

The dancers stand in a straight line at equi-distant stations,
alternately facing up and down, thus : —

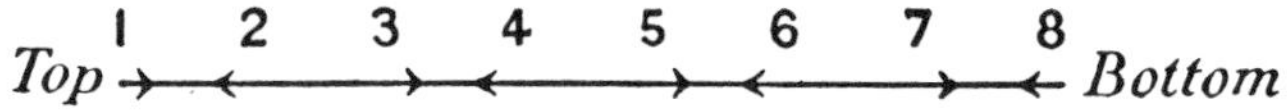

DIAGRAM 8.

Odd numbers face down ; even numbers up. As in the
circular hey the dancers move at an even rate, and pass each
other alternately by the right and left. The movement is
shown in diagram 9, the dotted and unbroken lines indicating,
respectively, the upward and downward tracks described by
the dancers :—

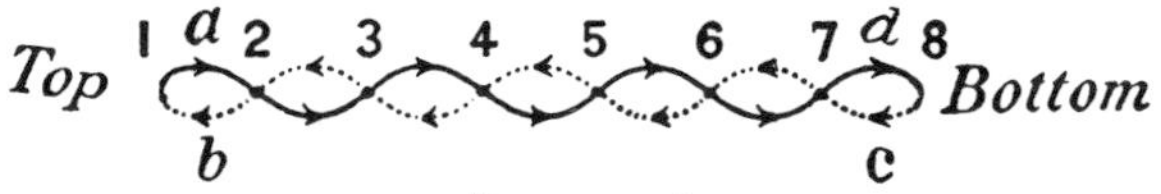

DIAGRAM 9.

It will be seen that the dancers after making the last pass
at either end make a whole-turn—bearing to the right if the

last pass was by the right, or to the left if the last pass was by the left—and re-enter the line, now in reverse direction, the first pass after re entrance being by the same shoulder, right or left, as the preceding one.

When the Straight-hey is performed by three dancers only, we have the form in which the hey occurs most frequently in the Country Dance. On this account it will perhaps be advisable to describe this particular case in detail.

THE STRAIGHT HEY-FOR-THREE.

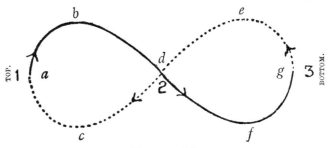

DIAGRAM 10.

No. 1 faces down, Nos. 2 and 3 up.

All simultaneously describe the figure eight, as shown in the above diagram, and return to places, passing along the unbroken line as they move down, and along the dotted line as they move up. At the beginning of the movement, therefore, No. 1 will dance along *a b*, No. 2 along *d c*, and No. 3 along *g e*, *i.e.*, Nos. 1 and 2 will pass by the right, Nos. 1 and 3 by the left.

In order that the dancers may not obstruct one another the two lobes of the figure should be made as broad as time and space will permit.

This is presumably the correct way in which the hey-for-three should be executed in the Country Dance, although we have no direct evidence that it was in fact so danced in Playford's day. Hogarth, however, in his *Analysis of Beauty* (1753), after defining the hey as "a cypher of S's, a number of serpentine lines interlacing and intervolving one another," prints a diagram of the hey-for-three which, although it might have been clearer, seems to show that the way the figure was danced at that period was substantially the same as that described above.

Moreover, Wilson (*The Analysis of Country Dancing,* 1811) also describes the figure and prints a diagram, of which the following—except that for clearness' sake the tracks are differentiated by means of varied lines—is a faithful reproduction :—

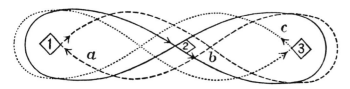

No. 1 moves along the broken line *a*; No. 2 along the line *b*; and No. 3 along the dotted line *c*.

Except that the two half heys are inverted—the two *lower* dancers beginning the movement and passing by the *left*—the method shown in the diagram is precisely the same as that we have above described.

The straight-hey may be performed progressively. It is unnecessary, however, to describe in detail the way in which this is effected, because, in principle, the method is the same as that already explained in Fig. 11.

Playford makes frequent use of the expressions "Single Hey" and "Double Hey." It is difficult to say with certainty what he means by these terms, because he uses them very loosely. Very often they are identical with what we have called the straight- and circular-hey. As, however, this is not always the case, I have, with some reluctance, substituted the terms used above, which are self-explanatory and free from ambiguity.

The figures above described are the commonplaces of the Country Dance, and are to be found, one or other of them, in pretty nearly every dance. The rest—and they are infinite in number and variety—are described in the notations as they occur.

THE TECHNIQUE OF FIGURE-DANCING.

The first requisite of the figure dancer, as has been already pointed out, is the capacity to move hither and thither, freely and easily, with complete control over direction and speed. Having attained this power he must then learn (1) to " time " his movements accurately ; (2) to phrase them in accord with the music ; (3) to blend them into one continuous movement without halts or hesitations ; and (4) to execute them in concert with his fellow-dancers.

Timing.— As the movements and the figures of the dance are but the translation, in terms of bodily action, of the music which accompanies them, the dancer when learning a dance should first of all listen carefully to the tune, and, if possible, memorise it. In particular he should note the number and relative lengths of its several phrases and calculate the number of steps that can be danced to each of them (two in every bar in duple, and three in triple-measure).

In the description of the dances given in the notation it will be found that a definite number of bars, and therefore of steps, is allotted to every figure and to every part of every figure, and it is by this system of measurement by step that the dancers " time " their movements with the music. Every dancer, therefore, must always have in mind not only the form and the shape of the figure he is executing, but the number of steps apportioned to the figure as a whole and to each subsidiary section of which that figure is compounded. So long, however, as he " times " his movements correctly and arrives at his appointed station at the end of each section of the figure, it is for him to determine the precise manner in which he shall distribute his steps in relation to the track or course described. He may, for instance, enlarge his track by taking larger steps, or restrict it by taking shorter ones. In the Gip, for example, the size of the circle described by the two dancers is immaterial so long as, by regulating their speed, they succeed in completing the circuit and regaining their original stations in the prescribed number of steps. When pressed for time the dancer may find it helpful to anticipate a movement, *i.e.*, to start it a beat or so in advance ; or *per contra* when he has time in hand, to delay it by taking one or more preliminary " balance-steps " before getting under way. Devices of this kind should, of course, be employed sparingly and never without good reason, as, for example, in the cases above cited, to avoid unseemly scurrying on the one hand or a premature conclusion on the other.

Phrasing.—It is just as necessary for the dancer to phrase his steps and movements as it is for the musician to phrase his notes and strains, or for the writer to punctuate his sentences. The purpose in each case is the same—to define and make intelligible what would otherwise be ambiguous or meaningless. A series of equally accented dance-steps, musical sounds, or verbal syllables, conveys no meaning until by the periodic recurrence of stronger accents the steps, sounds, or words, are separated into groups, co-ordinated, and some sort of relationship established between them.

The writer indicates these groups and their relative values by punctuation ; the speaker by pauses, emphasis of particular words, and by the rise and fall of his voice ; the musician by slurs or phrases, which define the positions of the rhythmical accents; while the dancer groups his steps in correspondence with the rhythmic phrases of the accompanying music. The dancer, like the musician, must be careful to distinguish between the metrical accents (*i.e.*, the accents or beats within the bar) and the rhythmical accents (of which the bar itself is the unit), the former corresponding to the " foot " in prosody, the latter to the " verse."

Technically, the dancer phrases his movements by gradating the accents which he imparts to his steps, giving the strongest accent ·to the first step of a group and the weakest to the last. The strength of the step accent depends partly upon foot-spring, but mainly upon body-balance. In a stationary figure like the turn-single, the step-accents are determined solely by the height and energy of the springs with which the steps are made. When, however, the dancer is in motion, the accent of the step depends less upon the strength of the spring forward than upon the momentum generated and controlled by the inclination of the body in the direction of motion. Before beginning a movement from rest, therefore, the dancer should throw his weight on to one foot and adjust the inclination of his body so that the first step of his phrase, which is always the most important, as it is also the strongest, may be made with the requisite emphasis.

The dancer must never make any movement in the dance, however insignificant, that is not phrased, *i.e.*, executed rhythmically in accord with the music. This injunction must be held to apply as much to arm-movements as to steps. For instance, in giving or taking a hand, he should begin the movement in plenty of time—two or three beats beforehand— and raise and move the arm in rhythm with the music.

Continuity. — The directions given in the notation are divided into Parts, figures, etc., only for the sake of clearness of description.   The aim of the dancer should be to conceal, not to call attention to these divisions.   In learning a dance it will probably be necessary to dissect its movements, to parse, so to speak, each component section ; but in the finished dance these subordinate elements must be pieced together and merged into one continuous movement as complete and organic in structure as the movements of a symphony.

To this end the dancer must think ahead, perceive the relation between that which he is at the moment doing with that which is to follow, so that he may give to the concluding cadence of each subsidiary phrase its just degree of emphasis, and pass on without hesitation to the movement that follows. If he fails in this, his movements will be spasmodic, his phrases isolated and unrelated, and his performance as a whole as unintelligible and difficult to follow as reading aloud by a child who spells out and pronounces with equal emphasis each word as he proceeds.

Concerted movement.—The performer in a concerted dance has not only to consider his own individual movements, but to relate them to those of his companions in the dance.   The expert figure-dancer is probably far more conscious of the movements of his fellow-dancers than of his own ; indeed, his pleasure, as well as theirs, depends very largely upon the completeness with which he effaces his own personality and loses himself in the dance.

Although the continuous and accurate adjustment of position by the dancer in a figure-dance is of first-rate importance, it is quite possible to exaggerate it, and by paying too much attention to precision of line and symmetry of figure, to stiffen and formalize the movements, and to give to the dance the appearance of a military drill.   The ideal is to steer a middle course.   To this end the following general directions will be found useful :--

In line formation each dancer should adjust his position in relation to the dancer on either side. In dual movements, *e.g.*, the Side, Arms, Back-to-back, etc., the distances traversed by each performer should be approximately equal. In the heys—especially the straight-hey-for-three—and the Gip, the performers should describe identically the same track. In the forming of rings the dancers should extend their arms and move round in a circle, edging towards the centre until they are near enough to link hands with the dancers on either side.

STYLE.

The foregoing explanations will, it is hoped, enable the reader to interpret the figures described in the notations that are presently to follow. The dancer should, however, be reminded that technical proficiency has no value except as an aid to artistic expression, and indeed, if it be not so used, the dance will never rise above the level of a physical exercise.

Although in the nature of things it is impossible to instruct the dancer how he may impart æsthetic significance to his physical movements, there are nevertheless certain general considerations to which his attention may profitably be directed. He can, for instance, turn his attention to Style, the cultivation of which will carry him a few steps at any rate along the right road. By style we do not mean polish, *i.e.*, perfected physical movement, but rather the air, the manner with which physical movements are executed. It is partly individual, the expression—that is, voluntary or involuntary—of the dancer's personality, and partly derived from the character of the dance itself.

Although the personal factor is inherent in every human action, and can never, therefore, be entirely eliminated therefrom, it may be, and often is, suppressed to the point where it becomes unconscious, as in walking and other common activities and habits. Now the folk-dance, owing to its corporate, unconscious origin, is essentially an impersonal dance, a unique instrument for the expression of those ideas and emotions that are held and felt collectively, but peculiarly unfitted for the exploitation of personal idiosyncrasies. The folk dance, therefore, is emphatically not the place for the display of those self-conscious airs and graces, fanciful posings and so forth, that play so large a part in dances of a more conventional order.

The dancer must therefore put these aside and seek elsewhere for material upon which to mould his style, and this he will find in the character of the dance itself. He should note that the Country Dance is less strenuous, less stern, and less detached than the Morris ; less involved and less intense than the Sword Dance ; but freer, jollier, more intimate, and, in a sense, more human than either—perhaps because it is the only one of the three in which both sexes take part. It is a mannered dance, gentle and gracious, formal in a simple, straightforward way, but above all gay and sociable. The spirit of merriment, however, although never wholly absent from the dance, is not always equally obvious. There are certain dances that are comparatively quiet and subdued in style, in which the normal gaiety is toned down to a decorous suavity ; while between dances of this kind and those of the more light-hearted variety, there are many that are emotionally intermediate in type. It should be the aim of the dancer to feel these temperamental differences, and reflect them in his manner and style.

The clue to these emotional variations he will, of course, find in the accompanying music. The dance is but the inter-pretation or translation, in terms of bodily action, of the music upon which it is woven, just as the melody of the song is primarily the expression of the text. Music moreover is the predominant partner of the union ; there can be no dance without music, This intimate relationship between the music and the dance and, in a sense, the subservience of the latter to the former, must always be present to the mind of the dancer. Not only must his rhythms accord with those of the music, as has already been pointed out, but his style, the character that he gives to his movements, must also be in harmony with the character of the music.

The application of this principle, viz., the subordination of the dance to the music, is imperative, especially in the case of the dances in the present volume. For the Playford dances, despite the number and variety of their figures, are very persistent in type, and were it not for the wide range of the emotional content of the tunes it would be difficult to give to them the necessary variety of treatment.

It should be added that any spectacular qualities that the Country Dance may possess are fortuitous, or, rather, the inevitable outcome of the perfect fashioning of means to end. Its beauty, being implicit, needs, therefore, no artificial embellishment. An elaborate theatrical setting would be as irrelevant and impertinent as for the dancers to deck themselves in rich and fanciful costumes. All that the dancers need is plenty of space, an even, non-slippery floor and dresses which will allow to the body and limbs complete freedom of action.

NOTATION.

JENNY PLUCK PEARS.

Round for six; in six parts (1st Ed., 1650).

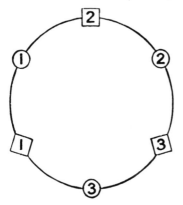

MUSIC.		MOVEMENTS.
		FIRST PART.
A1	1—4	Hands-six, eight slips clockwise.
	5—8	Partners set and turn single.
A2	1—4	Hands-six, eight slips counter-clockwise to places.
	5—8	Partners set and turn single.
B	1—2	First man, taking his partner by the right hand, sets her in the middle facing him.

JENNY PLUCK PEARS—*continued.*

MUSIC.		MOVEMENTS.
		FIRST PART— *continued.*
	3—4	Second man does the same with his partner.
	5—6	Third man the same.
	7—8	Partners honour each other.
		SECOND PART.
A1	1—8	Women stand in the middle back to back, while the men dance round them clockwise, not joining hands (sk.s.).
A2	1—8	Men dance round counter clockwise to places.
B	1—2	First man takes his partner by the left hand, and places her beside him.
	3—4	Second man does the same with his partner.
	5—6	Third man the same.
	7—8	Partners honour one another.
		THIRD PART.
A1	1—4	Partners side (r.s.).
	5—8	Partners set and turn single.
A2	1—8	All that again.
B	1—2	First woman takes her partner by the left hand and places him in the middle facing her.
	3—4	Second woman the same.
	5—6	Third woman the same.
	7—8	Partners honour each other.

JENNY PLUCK PEARS—*continued.*

MUSIC.		MOVEMENTS.
		FOURTH PART.
A1	1—8	Men stand in the middle of the ring, while the women dance round them clockwise, not joining hands (sk.s.).
A2	1—8	Same again, women dancing round, counter-clockwise, to places.
B	1—2	First woman takes her partner by the right hand and places him beside her.
	3—4	Second woman the same.
	5—6	Third woman the same.
	7—8	Partners honour each other.
		FIFTH PART.
A1	1—4	Partners arm with the right.
	5 - 8	Partners set and turn single.
A2	1—4	Partners arm with the left.
	5—8	Partners set and turn single.
B	1—8	Same as B in First Part.
		SIXTH PART.
A1, A2, & **B**		Same as in Second Part.

PUTNEY FERRY.

Round for six ; in three parts (4th Ed., 1670).

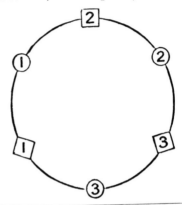

MUSIC.		MOVEMENTS.
		FIRST PART.
A	1—4	Hands-six, eight slips, clockwise.
	5—8	The same back again, counter-clockwise, to places.
B1	1—4	Men meet and hands-three once round clockwise, facing outward ; while women turn single twice round, clockwise and counter-clockwise.
	5—8	Men turn their partners.
B2	1—4	Women meet and hands-three once round clockwise, facing outward ; while men turn single twice round, clockwise and counter-clockwise.
	5—8	Men turn their partners.
C1	1—2	Each man sets to the woman on his left.
	3—4	Each man sets to the woman opposite him.
	5—6	Each man honours his partner.

PUTNEY FERRY—*continued.*

MUSIC.		MOVEMENTS.
		First Part – *continued.*
	7—8	Men turn their partners.
C2	1—2	Each woman sets to the man on her right.
	3—4	Each woman sets to the man opposite her.
	5—6	Women honour their partners.
	7—8	Men turn their partners.
		Second Part.
A	1—4	Partners side (r.s.).
	5—8	That again.
B1	1—8	Same as B2 in First Part.
B2	1—8	Same as B1 in First Part.
C1 and C2		Same as in First Part, the dancers folding their arms as they set.
		Third Part.
A	1—4	Partners arm with the right.
	5—8	Partners arm with the left.
B1 and B2		Same as in First Part.
C1 and C2		Same as in First Part, dancers wiping their eyes with their handkerchiefs as they set.

MAGE ON A CREE.*

Round for eight; in three parts (1st Ed., 1650).

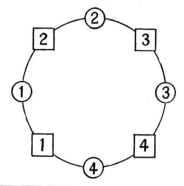

MUSIC.		MOVEMENTS.
		FIRST PART.
A1	1—4	All take hands, move forward a double, and fall back a double to places (r.s.).
	5—8	Partners set and turn single.
A2	1—8	All that again.
A3	1—4	Men hands-four once round to places, facing outward (sl.s.).
	5—8	Each man turns the woman on his left, *i.e.*, first man turns second woman, second man turns third woman, etc. (sk.s.).
A4	1—4	Women meet and hands-four once round to places, facing outward (sl.s.).
	5—8	Men turn their partners (sk.s.).

* In the 17th edition the title is "Madge on a Tree or Margery Cree."

MAGE ON A CREE—*continued.*

MUSIC.		MOVEMENTS.
		SECOND PART.
A1	1—4	Partners side (r.s.).
	5—8	Partners set and turn single.
A2	1—8	All that again.
A3	1—4	Men skip half-way round, clockwise, and fall into opposite places, each passing before the first woman on his left and behind the second.
	5—8	Women move forward a double, and fall back a double to places, turning single as they do so (r.s.).
A4	1—4	Men skip half-way round, clockwise to places, passing before the women on their left and behind their partners.
	5—8	Same as in A3.
		THIRD PART.
A1	1—4	Partners arm with the right.
	5—8	Partners set and turn single.
A2	1—8	Partners arm with the left, set, and turn single.
A3	1—4	Each man turns the woman on his left once round, and moves round one place clockwise (sk.s.).
	5—8	Each man turns the next woman once round, and moves round another place clockwise (sk.s.)
A4	1—8	Movement continued, as in A3, to places.

THE FINE COMPANION.

Round for eight ; in three parts (1st Ed., 1650).

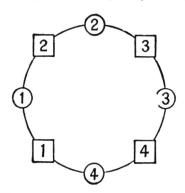

MUSIC.		MOVEMENTS.
		FIRST PART.
A1	1—4	All take hands, move forward a double and fall back a double to places (r.s.).
	5—8	Partners set and turn single.
A2	1—8	All that again.
B1	1—2	Men move forward and meet (r.s.).
	3—4	Women move forward and meet ; while men fall back to places (r.s.).
	5—8	Women fall back to places ; while men meet and hands-four once round to places.
B2	1—2	Women meet (r.s.).
	3—4	Men meet ; while women fall back to places (r.s.).
	5—8	Men fall back to places ; while women meet and hands-four once round to places.

THE FINE COMPANION—*continued.*

MUSIC.		MOVEMENTS.
		SECOND PART.
A1	1—4	Partners side.
	5—8	Partners set and turn single.
A2	1—8	All that again.
B1	1—2	First and third couples move forward and meet.
	3—4	Second and fourth couples meet; while first and third couples fall back to places.
	5—8	Second and fourth couples fall back to places; while first and third couples meet and hands-four once round to places.
B2	1—8	Same as B1, second and fourth couples meeting first.
		THIRD PART.
A1	1—4	Partners arm with the right.
	5—8	Partners set and turn single.
A2	1—4	Partners arm with the left.
	5—8	Partners set and turn single.
B1	1—8	Men meet and hands-four once round to places, facing outward (r.s.); while women skip round them counter-clockwise, not joining hands.
B2	1—8	Women meet and hands-four to places, facing outward (r.s.); while men skip round them to places, counter-clockwise, not joining hands.

NEWCASTLE.

Round for eight; in three parts (1st Ed , 1650).

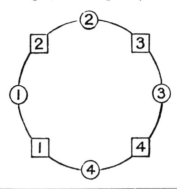

MUSIC.		MOVEMENTS.
		First Part.
A1	1—4	All take hands, move forward a double, and fall back a double to places (r.s.).
	5—6	Partners set to each other.
	7—8	Each man sets with the woman on his left.
A2	1—8	All that again.
B1	1—2	Partners link right arms and swing round once.
	3—8	Men left-hands-across, counter-clockwise, to places (r.s.); while women skip round them, clockwise, to places, not joining hands.
B2	1—2	Partners link left arms and swing round once (r.s.).
	3—8	Women right-hands across, clockwise, to places (r.s.); while men skip round them, counter-clockwise, to places, not joining hands.

Newcastle   *Round for eight*

Meet all, back againe, set to your owne, and to the next ∵ That againe ∴

Sides all with your owne, and change places • Sides with the next, and change places with them ——

Arms all with your We. and change places • Armes with the next and change places ∴ Now every man is with his owne Wo. in the Co. place.

Armes all with your owne by the right, men all fall with your left hands into the middle. We. go round them to your places ∴ Armes againe with your owne, and We. left hands in, men goe about them towards the left to your places ∴

The first man and 3. Wo. take hands and meet, the first Wo. and 3. man, lead out againe then holding up your hands, the other foure caſt off and come under your armes to their places ∵ The other foure the like ∵

Fall back from each other, foure and foure a breſt to each wall. turn and change places with your oppoſites ∵ Fall back from each other foure and foure along the roome, turne S. change places with your oppoſite ∴ So each falls into his place as at firſt.

NEWCASTLE— *continued.*

MUSIC.		MOVEMENTS.
		SECOND PART.
A1	1— 4	Partners side (r.s.).
	5—6	Partners go a single to the right and honour.
	7 – 8	Partners change places, passing by the left (r.s.).
A2	1 – 8	Same again, each man siding with the woman on his right, and changing places with her.
B1	1—4	First man and third woman lead forward a double, change hands, and lead back a double (r.s.) ; while third man and first woman do the same.
	5—8	First man and third woman hold up their arms and make an arch ; while third man and first woman do the same. Fourth man and fourth woman now cast off (the man to his right, the woman to her left), pass between first man and third woman and return to the same places ; while second man and second woman cast off in like manner, pass between third man and first woman and return to the same places.
B2	1—4	Second man and fourth woman lead forward a double, change hands, and lead back a double ; while fourth man and second woman do the same (r.s.).

NEWCASTLE—*continued.*

MUSIC.	MOVEMENTS.
	SECOND PART—*continued.*
5—8	Second man and fourth woman hold up their arms and make an arch; while fourth man and second woman do the same. First man and first woman now cast off (the man to his right, the woman to her left), pass between second man and fourth woman and return to the same places; while third man and third woman, casting off in like manner, pass between fourth man and second woman and return to the same places.
	THIRD PART.
A1 1—8	Each man arms with the right, and then with the left, with the woman on his right, and changes places with her.
A2 1—8	Each man arms with the right, then with the left, with the next woman on his right, and changes places with her. (Partners are now side by side, but in opposite places.)
B1 1—4	Second couple joins hands with first man and third woman, and all four face the right wall; while fourth couple joins hands with third man and first woman, and all four face the left wall. Standing thus, all fall back a double and then move forward a double (r.s.).

NEWCASTLE—*continued.*

MUSIC.	MOVEMENTS.
	THIRD PART—*continued.*
5—8	All turn single. Each man changes places with the woman opposite.
B2 1—4	First couple joins hands with fourth man and second woman, and all four face up; while third couple joins hands with second man and fourth woman, and all four face down. Standing thus, all fall back a double and move forward a double (r.s.).
5—8	All turn single and change places with the opposites, passing by the right (r.s.).

GATHERING PEASCODS.

Round for as many as will; in three parts (1st Ed., 1650).

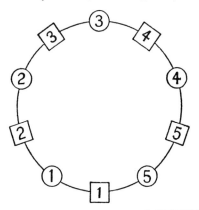

MUSIC.		MOVEMENTS.
		FIRST PART.
A1	1—4	Hands-all eight slips clockwise.
	5—6	All turn single.
A2	1—4	Hands-all eight slips counter-clockwise.
	5—6	All turn single.
B1	1—6	Men meet; hands-all to places.
B2	1—6	Women the same.
C1	1—2	Men move forward a double and meet, clapping their hands on the first beat of the second bar (r.s.).
	3—4	Women move forward a double, clapping hands on the first beat of the fourth bar; while men fall back to places (r.s.).

GATHERING PEASCODS—*continued.*

MUSIC.		MOVEMENTS.
		FIRST PART—*continued.*
	5 – 6	Men meet as before, clapping hands on the first beat of the sixth bar ; while women fall back to places (r.s.).
	7—8	Men fall back to places, turning single as they do so.
C2	1—2	Women meet, clapping hands on the first beat of second bar (r.s.).
	3—4	Men meet, clapping hands on the first beat of the fourth bar; while women fall back to places (r.s.).
	5—6	Women meet, clapping hands on the first beat of the sixth bar; while men fall back to places (r.s.).
	7—8	Women fall back to places, turning single as they go.
		SECOND PART.
A1	1 – 4	Partners side (r.s.).
	5—6	All turn single.
A2	1—6	All that again.
B1	1—6	Women meet ; hands-all to places.
B2	1—6	Men the same.
C1	1—8	Same as C2 in First Part.
C2	1—8	Same as in C1 in First Part.

GATHERING PEASCODS—*continued.*

MUSIC.	MOVEMENTS.
	THIRD PART.
A1 1—4	Partners arm with the right.
5—6	All turn single.
A2 1—4	Partners arm with the left.
5— 6	All turn single.
B1 and **B2**	The same as in First Part.
C1 and **C2**	The same as in First Part.

ORANGES AND LEMONS.
Square for eight; in three parts (3rd Ed., 1665).

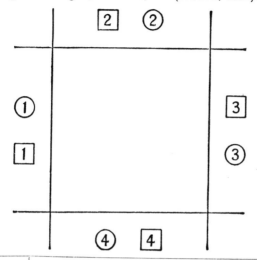

MUSIC.		MOVEMENTS.
		FIRST PART.
A	1—4	All move forward a double, meet, and fall back a double to places.
	5—8	That again.
B1	Bar 1	Men honour their partners.
	Bar 2	Men honour the women on their left.
	3—6	Men hands-four, half-way round, clockwise, and fall into opposite places (r.s.).
	Bar 7	Women honour the men on their left.
	Bar 8	Women honour the men on their right.
	9—12	Women hands-four, half-way round clockwise, and fall each beside her partner (r.s.).

ORANGES AND LEMONS—*continued.*

MUSIC.		MOVEMENTS.
		FIRST PART—*continued.*
B2	Bar 1	Men honour their partners.
	Bar 2	Men honour the women on their left.
	3—6	Men hands-four, half-way round counter-clockwise, to places (r.s.).
	Bar 7	Women honour the men on their left.
	Bar 8	Women honour the men on their right.
	9—12	Women hands-four, half-way round counterclockwise, and fall into their own places beside their partners (r.s.).
		SECOND PART.
A	1—4	Partners side (w.s.).
	5—8	That again.
B1	Bar 1	Partners take right hands, raise them, and move a single to the right.
	Bar 2	Partners take left hands, raise them, and move a single to the left.
	3—6	The circular hey (Fig. 10, p. 49); partners giving right hands to each other, and then left to the next (two changes) (r.s.).
	7—12	Movement continued as in bars 1—6, all moving round one place more.
B2	1—12	Movement continued, as in B1, to places.

ORANGES AND LEMONS—*continued.*

MUSIC.	MOVEMENTS.
	THIRD PART.
A 1—4	Partners arm with the right.
5—8	Partners arm with the left, and first and third men lead their partners forward to face second and fourth couples respectively.
B1 Bar 1	First and second couples honour each other; while third and fourth couples do the same.
Bar 2	Partners honour each other.
3—6	First and second couples hands-four, half-way round, while third and fourth couples do the same. Second and fourth couples, men leading their partners, fall back into first and third couples' places respectively; simultaneously first and third couples lead forward and face fourth and second couples (*i.e.*, second and fourth couples move on one place counter-clockwise and take up positions facing centre; while first and third couples move on one place clockwise and take up positions with their backs to the centre).
Bar 7	First and fourth couples honour each other; while second and third couples do the same.
Bar 8	Partners honour each other.
9—12	First and fourth couples hands-four, half-way round; while second and third couples do the same. Movement continued as in Bars 3—6.
B2 1—12	Movement continued, as in B1, to places.

DULL SIR JOHN.

Square for eight; in three parts (1st Ed., 1650).

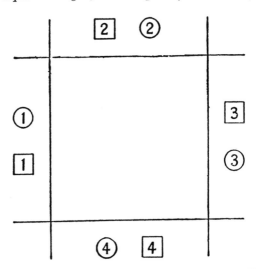

MUSIC.		MOVEMENTS.
		FIRST PART.
A1	1—2	First man leads forward first woman (w.s.).
	3—4	First man passes between second man and second woman, turns to his left, and returns behind the second woman to his place; while first woman passes between fourth man and fourth woman, turns to her right, and returns behind fourth man to her place (r.s.).
	5—8	The third couple the same; the man passing between fourth man and fourth woman, the woman between second man and second woman.
A2	1—4	The second couple the same; the man passing between third man and third woman, the woman between first man and first woman.

DULL SIR JOHN—*continued.*

MUSIC.		MOVEMENTS.

FIRST PART—*continued.*

	5—8	The fourth couple the same; the man passing between first man and first woman, the woman between third man and third woman.
B1	1—2	First and third men cross over and change places (r.s.).
	3—4	First and third women the same (r.s.).
	5—8	First and third couples right-hands across, half-way round to places (sk.s.).
B2	1—8	Second and fourth couples the same; second and fourth men stand each behind his partner.

SECOND PART.

A1	1—4	First man passes between second man and woman, and takes third woman's place; while first woman passes between fourth man and fourth woman into third man's place (r.s.).
		Simultaneously, third man and third woman cross over and take, respectively, first woman's and first man's places (r.s.).
	5—8	Third man passing between fourth man and fourth woman returns to his place; while third woman passing between second man and second woman does the same (r.s.).

DULL SIR JOHN—*continued.*

MUSIC.		MOVEMENTS.
		SECOND PART—*continued.*
		Simultaneously, first man and first woman cross over into their places (r.s.).
		First and third men then stand behind their respective partners.
A2	1—8	The second and fourth couples do the same as first and third couples in A1.
B1	1—8	First and third couples, standing in single file, dance the straight-hey (Fig. 12, p. 53), the first and third woman first meeting and passing by the right (eight changes).
B2	1—8	Second and fourth couples do the same.
		THIRD PART.
A1	1—4	The four men turn outward, each to his left, and, passing behind their partners, move round one place, counter-clockwise.
	5—8	The four women turn outward, each to her right, and move round one place, clockwise.
A2	1—4	Men move round counter-clockwise another place.
	5—8	Women do the same, clockwise.

DULL SIR JOHN—*continued.*

MUSIC.		MOVEMENTS.

THIRD PART—*continued.*

(Partners now stand side by side, first and third couples in each other's places, and second and fourth couples the same.)

B1 1—4 First and thir men go back-to-back with their opposites, passing by the right (r.s.).

5—6 First man and third woman meet, take right hands and change places; while third man and first woman do the same (r.s.).

7—8 First and third men take their partners by the left hand and change places (r.s.). (First and third couples are now in their own places.)

B2 1—8 Second and fourth couples do the same as first and third couples in B1.

RUFTY TUFTY.

For four; in three parts (1st Ed., 1650).

2	②
①	1

MUSIC.	MOVEMENTS.
	FIRST PART.
A 1—4	Both couples move forward a double, meet, and fall back a double to places (r.s.).
5—8	That again.
B 1—4	Partners set and turn single.
5—8	That again.
C 1—2	First man, with his left hand, leads his partner a double toward the left wall; while second man, with his left hand, leads his partner a double toward the right wall (r.s.).
3—4	Both couples turn round and face each other; the men, with their right hands, lead their partners a double to places (r.s.).
5—6	All turn single.
7—10	First man, with his right hand, leads second woman up a double, turns round and, with his left hand, leads her down a double to her place; while second man, with his right hand, leads first woman down a double, turns round and, with his left hand, leads her up a double to her place (r.s.).
11—12	All turn single.

RUFTY TUFTY—*continued.*

MUSIC.		MOVEMENTS.
		SECOND PART.
A	1—4	Partners side with each other.
	5—8	That again.
B	1—8	The same as B in First Part
C	1—12	The same as C in First Part.
		THIRD PART.
A	1—4	Partners arm with the right.
	5—8	Partners arm with the left.
B	1—8	Same as B in First Part.
C	1—12	Same as C in First Part.

PARSON'S FAREWELL.

For four; in three parts (1st Ed., 1650).

MUSIC.		MOVEMENTS.
		FIRST PART.
	1—2	Couples advance a double and meet (w.s.).
	3—4	First man and first woman move sideways four slips up; while second man and second woman move sideways four slips down.
	5—6	All fall back a double (w.s.).
	7—8	First man and first woman move sideways four slips down; while second man and second woman move sideways four slips up, to places.
B1	1—2	The two men rise on the first beat of the bar (*i.e.*, standing with feet parallel and close together, they rise on the toes of both feet and then lower the heels to the ground). The two women rise on the first beat of the second bar.
	3—4	All rise four times, on the first and middle beats of each bar.
	5—8	First man turns second woman; while second man turns first woman.
B2	1—2	The two women rise on the first beat of the first bar. The two men rise on the first beat of the second bar.
	3—8	The same as in B1.

PARSON'S FAREWELL—*continued.*

MUSIC.		MOVEMENTS.
		SECOND PART.
A	1—2	Couples move forward a double and meet (w.s.).
	3—4	First man leads second woman up a double; while second man leads first woman down a double (r.s.).
	5—6	All four turn round, face in the opposite direction, and change hands. First man then leads second woman down a double; while the second man leads first woman up a double (r.s.).
	7—8	All release hands and partners fall back to places, holding right hands.
B1	Bar 1	The two men meet (sk.s.), and take right hands.
	Bar 2	Releasing right hands, they clasp left hands.
	3—4	First man passes second man by the left, turns second woman with his right hand and moves into second man's place; while second man turns first woman with his right hand and moves into first man's place (sk.s.).
	5—6	The two men meet again, clasp right, and then left hands.
	7—8	Passing each other, by the left, first man turns his partner with his right hand and returns to his place; while second man does the same (sk.s.).

PARSON'S FAREWELL—*continued.*

MUSIC.	MOVEMENTS.
	SECOND PART—*continued.*
B2 Bar 1	The two women meet (sk.s.), and clasp left hands.
Bar 2	They release left and join right hands.
3—4	First woman, passing second woman by the right, turns second man with her left hand and moves into second woman's place; while second woman turns first man with her left hand and moves into first woman's place (sk.s.).
5—6	The two women meet (sk.s.), clasp left hands and then right.
7—8	Passing each other by the right, each woman turns her partner with her left hand and moves into her place (sk s.).
	THIRD PART.
A 1—2	The two men face their partners, take them by both hands, move sideways four slips toward each other, and meet.
3—4	First man faces second woman, takes her by both hands and moves sideways four slips up; while second man faces first woman, takes her by both hands and moves sideways four slips down.
5—6	The same couples move sideways four slips towards each other and meet.

PARSON'S FAREWELL—*continued.*

MUSIC.		MOVEMENTS.
		THIRD PART—*continued.*
	7—8	First man takes his partner by the right hand and falls back to his place; while second man does the same with his partner (w.s.).
B1	1—2	First man turns his partner with his right hand; while second man does the same with his partner (sk.s.).
	3—4	The two men cross over and change places (sk.s.).
	5—8	Partners face, and all dance the circular-hey (two changes) (Fig. 10, p. 49) (sk.s.); whereupon each man turns his partner half-way round and changes places with her.
B2	1—2	First and second men turn their partners with left hands.
	3—4	The two women cross over and change places, passing by the left (sk.s.).
	5—8	Partners face, and all dance the circular-hey (two changes) (sk.s.); whereupon each man turns his partner half-way round and changes places with her.

THE GLORY OF THE WEST.

For four; in three parts (1st Ed., 1650).

2　　②

①　　1

MUSIC.		MOVEMENTS.
		FIRST PART.
A	1—2	Both couples move forward a double and meet (r.s.).
	3—4	Both couples fall back a double to places (r.s.).
	5—6	Both couples fall back a double (r.s.).
	7—8	Both couples move forward a double to places.
B1	1—2	Men fall back a double; while women turn single (r.s.).
	3—4	Women fall back a double; while men turn single (r.s.).
	5—6	Men cross over and change places (r.s.).
	7—8	Women do the same.
	9—10	Hands-four, half-way round, to places.
B2	1—10	Same as B1.

THE GLORY OF THE WEST—*continued.*

MUSIC.		MOVEMENTS.
		SECOND PART.
A	1—4	First man and second woman side; while second man and first woman do the same (w.s.).
	5—8	Partners side with each other (w.s.).
B1	1—-2	Men turn outward, each to his left, and stand back-to-back behind their respective partners (r.s.).
	3—5	First man and first woman, standing back-to-back, turn round, counter-clockwise, to places (sl.s.); while second man and second woman do the same.
	6—7	Women turn outward, each to her right, and fall back-to-back behind their respective partners (r.s.).
	8—10	First woman and first man, standing back-to-back, turn round, clockwise, to places (sl.s.); while second woman and second man do the same.
B2	1—4	All move round in a ring, clockwise, to places (without handing), facing in the direction in which they move (r.s.).
	5—10	Right - hands - across, once round, to places (sk.s.).

THE GLORY OF THE WEST—*continued.*

MUSIC.		MOVEMENTS.
		THIRD PART.
A	1—4	First man and second woman arm with the right ; while second man and first woman do the same (r.s.).
	5—8	Partners arm with the left (r.s.).
B1	1—2	The two women meet (w.s.), and make an arch with their right arms.
	3—5	The two men meet under the arch and pass by the right ; each man then turns to his left, moves round and outside the other's partner, and returns to his place (sk.s.).
	6 – 7	The two men meet, and make an arch with their right arms (r.s.).
	8—10	The two women meet under the arch and pass by the left ; each woman then turns to her right, moves round and outside the other's partner, and returns to her place (sk.s.).
B2	1—2	First man and second woman meet, take right hands, pass and change places; while second man and first woman do the same (r.s.).
	3—4	Partners meet, take left hands, pass and change places (r.s.).
	5—8	Hands-four, half-way round, to places.
	9—10	All face up and, standing in line, first couple on the left, honour the Presence.

SAINT MARTIN'S.

For four; in three parts (1st Ed., 1650).

$$\boxed{2} \qquad ②$$

$$① \qquad \boxed{1}$$

MUSIC.		MOVEMENTS.
		FIRST PART.
A1	1—2	Both couples move forward a double and meet (w.s.).
	3—4	First man and first woman move sideways two slips up and two slips back again; while the second man and second woman move sideways two slips down and two slips back again.
	5—6	All turn single, the men counter-clockwise, the women clockwise.
	7—8	All turn single, men clockwise, women counter-clockwise, to places.
A2	1—4	The two couples cross over and change places (r.s.).
	5—6	Partners change places (r.s.).
	7—8	All turn single.
B1	1—2	Men fall back a double (r.s.); while women turn single.
	3—4	The two men move forward and meet, take left hands and change places (r.s.).

SAINT MARTIN'S—*continued.*

MUSIC.		MOVEMENTS.
		FIRST PART—*continued.*
	5—8	First man turns second woman once-and-a-half round with his right hand and changes places with her; while second man does the same with first woman (sk.s.).
B2	1—2	The two women fall back a double (r.s.); while men turn single.
	3—4	The two women move forward and meet, take left hands, and change places (r.s.).
	5—8	Partners turn once-and-a-half round with right hands and change places (sk.s.).
		SECOND PART.
A1	1—4	Couples take two steps backward and then cross over and change places (r.s.).
	5—8	Partners set and turn single.
A2	1—8	All that again.
B1	Bar 1	The two men meet and stand face to face (r.s.).
	Bar 2	The two women do the same (r.s.).
	3—6	Hands-four, half-way round (sl.s.).
	7—8	All turn single.
B2	Bar 1	The two women meet and stand face to face (r.s.).

SAINT MARTIN'S—*continued.*

MUSIC.	MOVEMENTS.
	SECOND PART—*continued.*
Bar 2	The two men do the same (r.s.).
3—6	Hands-four, half-way round to places (sl.s.).
7—8	All turn single.
	THIRD PART.
A1 1—2	Both couples move forward a double and meet (r.s.). Each man takes the woman opposite by both hands.
3—4	First man and second woman move sideways two slips up and then two slips back again; while second man and first woman move sideways two slips down and then two slips back again.
5—8	Both men cast off by the left, and, followed by their partners, return up the middle to places (r.s.).
A2 1—2	All fall back a double (r s.).
3—4	Partners change places (r.s.).
5—8	The two men meet, pass by the left, and fall back to their proper places; while—immediately after the men have passed each other—the two women meet, pass by the right, and fall back to their proper places (r.s.).

SAINT MARTIN'S—*continued.*

MUSIC.		MOVEMENTS.
		THIRD PART—*continued.*
B1	1—2	Men honour their partners.
	3—4	Women honour their partners.
	5—8	Right-hands-across, once round clockwise, to places (r.s.).
B2	1—2	Women honour their partners.
	3—4	Men honour their partners.
	5—6	Left hands-across, half-way round counter-clockwise (r.s.).
	7—8	All face up in line (first couple on the right), move forward a double and honour the Presence (r.s.).

HEY, BOYS, UP GO WE.

For four; in three parts (1st Ed., 1650).

MUSIC.		MOVEMENTS.
		FIRST PART.
A	1—4	Couples move forward a double and fall back a double to places (r.s.).
	5—8	That again.
B1	1—4	First man and second woman whole-gip facing outward, clockwise (Fig. 9, p. 48); while second man and first woman do the same (r.s.).
	5—8	First man and second woman whole-gip facing centre, counter-clockwise (Fig. 8, p. 47); while second man and first woman do the same (r.s.).
B2	1—4	First man and first woman whole-gip facing outward, clockwise; while second man and second woman do the same (r.s.).
	5—8	First man and first woman whole-gip facing centre, counter-clockwise; while second man and second woman do the same (r.s.).

HEY, BOYS, UP GO WE—*continued.*

MUSIC.		MOVEMENTS.
		SECOND PART.
A	1—4	Partners side (r.s.).
	5—8	First man and second woman side, while second man and first woman do the same.
B1	1— 2	Two men change places (r.s.).
	3—4	Two women do the same.
	5—8	Hands-four once round.
B2	1—2	Two women change places (r.s.).
	3—4	Two men do the same.
	5—8	Hands-four once round to places.
		THIRD PART.
A	1—4	Partners arm with the right.
	5—8	First man and second woman arm with the left; while second man and first woman do the same.
B1	1—4	First man and second woman, and second man and first woman half-pousette (r.s.), and change places (Fig. 6, p. 45).

HEY, BOYS, UP GO WE—*continued.*

MUSIC.	MOVEMENTS.
	THIRD PART—*continued.*
5—8	First man turns outward to his right and, followed by his partner, casts off and returns up the middle to the same place ; while second man casts off to his right and, followed by his partner, does the same (r.s.).
B2 1—4	Same as B1 to places (r.s.).
5—8	Same as B1, each man casting off to his left and, followed by his partner, returning up the middle to his place (r.s.).

GRIMSTOCK.

Longways for six; in three parts (2nd Ed., 1652).

$$\boxed{1} \qquad \boxed{2} \qquad \boxed{3}$$

$$\textcircled{1} \qquad \textcircled{2} \qquad \textcircled{3}$$

MUSIC.		MOVEMENTS.
		FIRST PART.
A1	1—4	All lead up a double and fall back a double to places (r.s.).
	5—8	Partners set and turn single.
A2	1—8	All that again.
B	Bar 1	First and second couples change places, first couple going down between the second (sk.s.).
	Bar 2	First and third couples change places, third couple coming up between the first (sk.s.).
	3—4	Second and third couples change places, second couple going down between the third (sk.s.).
	Bar 5	First and second couples change places, first couple coming up between the second (sk.s.).
	Bar 6	First and third couples change places, third couple going down between the first (sk.s.).
	7—8	Second and third couples change places, second couple coming up between the third (sk.s.).

GRIMSTOCK—*continued.*

MUSIC.		MOVEMENTS.
		SECOND PART.
A1	1—4	Partners side (r.s.).
	5—8	Partners set and turn single.
A2	1—8	All that again.
B	1—8	Same as B in First Part, partners facing each other with both hands joined (sl.s.).
		THIRD PART.
A1	1—4	Partners arm with the right.
	5—8	Partners set and turn single.
A2	1—8	Partners arm with the left, set and turn single.
B	Bar 1	First man changes places with first woman, passing by the left (sk.s.).
	2—4	Half the Straight hey-for-three (Fig. 12, p. 54) on each side (sk.s.).
	Bar 5	First man changes places with first woman, passing by the right (sk.s.).
	6—8	Half the Straight hey-for-three on each side to places (sk.s.).

THE BEGGAR BOY.

Longways for six; in three parts (1st Ed., 1650).

| 1 | 2 | 3 |

| (1) | (2) | (3) |

MUSIC.		MOVEMENTS.
		FIRST PART.
A	1—4	All lead up a double and fall back a double to places (r.s.).
	5—8	That again.
B1	1—4	First and third men face the left wall, move forward a double, and fall back a double to places; while first and third women face the right wall and do the same (r.s.). Simultaneously, second man and second woman advance a double and fall back a double to places (r.s.).
	5—8	Men hands-three, once round; while the women do the same on their own side.
B2	1—8	Same as B1.

THE BEGGAR BOY—*continued.*

MUSIC.		MOVEMENTS.
		SECOND PART.
A	1—4	Partners side (w.s.).
	5—8	That again.
B1	1—4	First couple faces down and third couple up; they change places, the first couple passing between the third man and the third woman; while the second man and the second woman fall back a double and move forward a double to places (r.s.).
	5—8	Third and second couples hands-four, once round; while first man and first woman set and turn single.
B2	1—8	Repeat B1, to places.
		THIRD PART.
A	1—4	Partners arm with the right.
	5—8	Partners arm with the left.
B1	1—4	All fall back a double and then move forward a double to places (r.s.).
	5—8	Men the half-hey (Fig. 12, p. 53); while the women do the same on their own side (r.s.).
B2	1—8	Repeat B1, to places.

JP. p.71

CHESTNUT; or DOVE'S FIGARY.

Longways for six ; in three parts (1st Ed., 1650).

MUSIC.		MOVEMENTS.
		FIRST PART.
A	1—4	All lead up a double and fall back a double to places (r.s.).
	5—8	That again.
B1	Bar 1	All, facing front, fall back two small steps (r.s.).
	2—4	Partners cross over and change places (r.s.).
	5—8	Men hands-three on the women's side, second man facing inward ; while women do the same on the men's side.
B2	1—8	Repeat B1, to places.
		SECOND PART.
A	1—4	Partners side.
	5—8	Partners arm with the left.
B1	1—4	Same as B1 in First Part.
	5—8	Men the half-hey (Fig. 12, p. 53) on the women's side ; while women do the same on the men's side (r.s.).
B2	1—8	Repeat B1, to places.

CHESTNUT; or DOVE'S FIGARY—*continued.*

MUSIC.		MOVEMENTS.
		THIRD PART.
A	1—4	Partners arm with the right.
	5—8	Partners arm with the left.
B1	1—4	Same as B1 in First Part.
	5—8	First couple leads down the middle to the last place, followed by second and third couples (w.s.).
B2	1—4	Same as B1 in First Part.
	5—8	First man, followed by second and third men, casts off and returns to his place; while first woman, followed by second and third women, casts off and returns to her place (r.s.).

THE BLACK NAG.

Longways for six; in three parts (4th Ed., 1670).

1	2	3
①	②	③

MUSIC.		MOVEMENTS.
		FIRST PART.
A	1—4	All lead up a double and fall back a double to places (r.s.).
	5—8	That again.
B1	1—2	First man and first woman face each other, take both hands, and dance four slips up.
	3—4	Second couple the same.
	5—6	Third couple the same.
	7—8	All turn single.
B2	1—2	Third man and third woman take both hands and dance four slips back to places.
	3—4	Second couple the same.
	5—6	First couple the same.
	7—8	All turn single.

THE BLACK NAG—*continued.*

MUSIC.		MOVEMENTS.
		SECOND PART.
A	1—4	Partners side (r.s.).
	5—8	That again.
B1	1—2	First man changes places with third woman, right shoulders foremost, passing back-to-back (sl.s.).
	3—4	First woman changes places with third man in like manner (sl.s.).
	5—6	Second man changes places with second woman in like manner (sl.s.).
	7—8	All turn single.
B2	1—8	All that again to places.
		THIRD PART.
A	1—4	Partners arm with the right.
	5—8	Partners arm with the left.
B1	1—8	Men the straight hey-for-three (Fig. 12, p. 53) on their own side (sk.s.).
B2	1—8	Women the straight hey-for-three on their own side (sk.s.).

CHEERILY AND MERRILY.

Longways for eight; in six parts (1st Ed., 1650).

| 1 | 2 | 3 | 4 |
| (1) | (2) | (3) | (4) |

MUSIC.		MOVEMENTS.
		FIRST PART.
A	1—4	All lead up a double and fall back a double to places (r.s.).
	5—8	That again.
B	1—4	Partners set and turn single.
	5—8	That again.
		SECOND PART.
A	1—2	Second man and third woman cross and change places (r.s.).
	3—4	Third man and second woman do the same.
	5—8	First and third couples hands-four once round; while second and fourth couples do the same.
B	1—2	Second man and third woman cross and change places (r.s.).
	3—4	Third man and second woman do the same.
	5—8	First and second couples hands-four once round; while third and fourth couples do the same.

CHEERILY AND MERRILY—*continued.*

MUSIC.		MOVEMENTS.
		SECOND PART.
A	1—4	Partners side (r.s.).
	5—8	That again.
B	1—4	Partners set and turn single.
	5—8	That again.
		FOURTH PART.
A	1—4	First and fourth men and women move forward a double and meet their partners; whereupon, first and fourth couples meet, the former leading down, the latter up (r.s.). Simultaneously, second and third men and second and third women fall back a double and then dance four slips, the second couple up and the third down.
	5—8	First and fourth couples hands-four once round; while second and third men turn their partners.
B	1—4	Second and third men and women move forward a double and meet their partners; whereupon, second and third couples meet, the former leading down, the latter up (r.s.). Simultaneously, first and fourth men and first and fourth women fall back a double and then dance four slips, the first couple up and the fourth down.
	5—8	Second and third couples hands-four once round; while first and fourth men turn their partners.

CHEERILY AND MERRILY—*continued.*

MUSIC.		MOVEMENTS.
		FIFTH PART.
A	1—4	Partners arm with the right.
	5—8	Partners arm with the left.
B	1—4	Partners set and turn single.
	5—8	That again.
		SIXTH PART.
A	1—4	Men hands-four.
	5—8	Women the same.
B	1—8	Men the straight-hey (Fig. 12, p. 53) on their own side; while women do the same.

TEN POUND LASS.

Longways for eight; in three parts (4th Ed., **1670**),
standing thus :—

MUSIC.		MOVEMENTS.
		FIRST PART.
A	1—4	Facing front, all fall back a double and move forward a double to places (r.s.).
	5—8	All lead up a double and fall back a double to places (r.s.).
B1	1—4	All face left wall and move forward (r.s.).
	5—8	All face front. Partners cross over and change places (r.s.).
B2	1—4	All face right wall and move forwards (r.s.).
	5—8	All face front. Partners cross over and change places (r.s.).
		SECOND PART.
A	1—4	Partners side (r.s.).
	5—8	That again.
B1	1—4	First and fourth couples meet (r.s.)—the first couple moving down, the fourth up—and hands-four once round; while second and

TEN POUND LASS—*continued.*

MUSIC.		MOVEMENTS.
		SECOND PART—*continued.*
		third men and second and third women fall back a double (r.s.), and then dance four slips, the second couple up, the third down, to top and bottom places, respectively.
	5—8	Partners set and turn single.
B2	1—4	Second and third couples meet (r.s.)—the second moving down, the third up—and hands-four once round to places; while first and fourth men and first and fourth women fall back a double, and dance four slips, the first couple up, and the fourth down, to places.
	5—8	Partners set and turn single.
		THIRD PART.
A	1—4	Partners arm with the right.
	5—8	Partners arm with the left.
B1	1—4	Partners cross over and change places (r.s.).
	5—8	First and second men and third and fourth women, hands-four, half-way round; while first and second women, third and fourth men do the same.
B2	1—4	Partners cross over and change places (r.s.).
	5—8	Same as in B1, to places.

NONESUCH; or, A LA MODE DE FRANCE.

Longways for eight; in five parts (1st Ed., 1650).

MUSIC.		MOVEMENTS.
		FIRST PART.
A1	1—4	All lead up a double and fall back a double to places (r.s.).
	5—8	That again.
B1	1—4	Partners set and turn single.
	5—8	That again.
		SECOND PART.
		(Duple minor-set.)
A1	1—4	First man and first woman face and move forward two steps; joining hands, they slip down between second man and second woman; releasing hands, first man turns clockwise to face second man, while first woman turns counter-clockwise to face second woman.
	5—8	First man takes second man by both hands and pushes him obliquely upward and outward four steps, and then draws backward four steps, leaving second man in the top place, he himself falling into the second place (r.s.); simultaneously, first and second women do the same (progressive).

NONESUCH; or, A LA MODE DE FRANCE *—continued.*

MUSIC.		MOVEMENTS.
		SECOND PART—*continued.*
B1	1—4	All four, facing front, fall back a double and move forward a double (r.s.).
	5—8	First and second men turn their partners.
		THIRD PART.
A1	1—2	Partners side to the right (r.s.).
	3—4	All turn single.
	5—6	Partners side to the left (r.s.).
	7—8	All turn single.
B1	Bar 1	First man slips diagonally up and toward the right wall, and stands midway between the two lines, facing down.
	Bar 2	First women slips in front of her partner and stands facing him.
	3—4	Second man and second woman do the same.
	5—8	Third couple does the same; and then the fourth couple.

NONESUCH ; or, A LA MODE DE FRANCE—*continued.*

MUSIC.		MOVEMENTS.

FOURTH PART.

A1 1—4   Partners arm with the right.

5—8   Partners arm with the left.

B1 1—4   Men dance four slips towards the right wall and four slips back again ; while women dance four slips towards the left wall, and four slips back again.

5—8   Men dance four slips towards the left wall and four slips back again; while women dance four slips towards the right wall, and four slips back again.

FIFTH PART.

A1 Bar 1   First man slips down and towards the left wall in his original place, and faces front.

Bar 2   First woman slips, in like manner, into her own place.

3—4   Second man does the same ; then second woman.

5—8   Third couple the same ; then the fourth.

B1 and **B2**   The progressive circular-hey, all handing as they pass (r.s.). First man and first woman begin the movement by passing each other by the right, and, upon completing one circuit, stay in their places while the rest finish the figure (Fig. 11, p. 51).

DARGASON; or, SEDANY.

For as many as will, in three parts (2nd Ed., 1652), standing thus:—

.... ⑤ ④ ③ ② ① 1️⃣ 2️⃣ 3️⃣ 4️⃣ 5️⃣ .....

MUSIC.		MOVEMENTS.
		FIRST PART.
A1	1—4	First man and first woman side (r.s.).
	5—8	They set to each other.
	7—8	They pass each other, by the left, turning single as they do so, the man clockwise, the woman counter-clockwise.
A2	1—8	First man and second woman side, set, turn single and pass each other, as in A1; while second man and first woman do the same.
A3	1—8	Same movements performed by three pairs of dancers, viz., first man and third woman, third man and first woman, and second man and second woman.
		These movements are performed as many times as there are couples, that is, until the first man and first woman reach, respectively, the bottom and top of the line. At the conclusion of the last of these repetitions, all the dancers make a half-turn, men clockwise and women counter-clockwise, and face in the reverse direction. This ends the first half of the figure.

DARGASON ; or, SEDANY—*continued.*

MUSIC.	MOVEMENTS.

First Part—*continued.*

In the second half of the figure the same movements are repeated, but in reverse order, the men moving and facing up, the women down. At the end of the first change (danced by the same pairs as the last change of the first half) the last man and the last woman, having reached their own places, remain there and take no further part in the performance of the figure. In each subsequent change two dancers, one at each end, will, in like manner, reach their own places and become neutral; so that upon the conclusion of the final repetition (danced by the first couple only) all the performers will be in their original places.

Second Part.

Same as the First Part, except that dancers, instead of siding, arm with the right in the first half of the movement, and with the left in the second half.

Third Part.

First, third, fifth, etc., men, and second, fourth, sixth, etc., women face down ; the rest face up.

Standing thus, all dance the straight-hey one complete circuit to places, handing as they pass (Fig. 12, p. 53).

GODDESSES.

Longways for as many as will; * in eleven parts
(1st Ed., 1650).

| 1 | 2 | 3 | 4 | . . . . . |
| 1 | 2 | 3 | 4 | . . . . . |

MUSIC.		MOVEMENTS.
		FIRST PART.
A	1—4	All lead up a double and fall back a double to places (r.s.).
	5—8	That again.
B	1—4	First man casts off and, followed by the rest of the men, casts down to the bottom place; while first woman, followed by the rest of the women, does the same (sk.s.).
	5—8	First man casts off and, followed by the rest of the men, casts up to his place; while the women do the same (sk.s.).
		SECOND PART.
A	1—4	First man crosses over and, followed by the rest of the men, casts down outside the women until he stands behind the last woman (sk.s.).
	5—8	Last man crosses over and, followed by the rest of the men, moves down to his place (sk.s.).
B	1—8	As in First Part.

* When there are more than four couples, it will be necessary to repeat each strain of the music throughout the dance, with the exception of the first strain, A, in the First Part.

GODDESSES—*continued.*

MUSIC.		MOVEMENTS.
		THIRD PART.
A	1—8	Women do as men did in Second Part (sk.s.).
B	1—8	As in First Part.
		FOURTH PART.
A	1—8	First man crosses over and, followed by the rest of the men, dances down outside the women, turns to his right below the last woman and dances up the middle to his place (sk.s.).
B	1—8	As in First Part.
		FIFTH PART.
A	1—8	Women do as men did in the Fourth Part (sk.s.).
B	1—8	As in First Part.
		SIXTH PART.
A	1—4	Men hands-all, clockwise.
	5—8	Men hands-all, counter-clockwise, to places.
B	1—8	As in First Part.
		SEVENTH PART.
A	1—8	Women do as men did in Sixth Part.
B	1—8	As in First Part.

GODDESSES—*continued*.

MUSIC		MOVEMENTS.
		EIGHTH PART.
A	1—4	Men and women hands-all, clockwise.
	5—8	All dance back again, counter-clockwise, to places.
B	1—8	As in First Part.
		NINTH PART.
A	1—8	Men dance the straight-hey on their own side, odd numbers facing down, even numbers up (sk.s.).　(Fig. 12, p. 53).
B	1—8	As in First Part.
		TENTH PART.
A	1—8	Women do as men did in the Ninth Part (sk.s.).
B	1—8	As in First Part.
		ELEVENTH PART.
A	*ad lib.*	All dance circular-hey (Fig. 10, p. 49), odd numbers facing up, even numbers down, first man and woman passing by the right (sk.s.).
B	1—8	As in First Part.

NEW BO-PEEP; or, PICKADILLA.

Longways for as many as will; in three parts
(1st Ed., 1650).

1	2	3	4	. . . . .
①	②	③	④	. . . . .

MUSIC.		MOVEMENTS.
		FIRST PART.
A	1—4	All lead up a double and fall back a double to places (r.s.).
	5—8	That again.
B1	1—2	Women turn round and face the right wall, and move forward a double (small skipping-steps).
	3—4	Men move forward a double toward right wall (r.s.). Each stands behind his partner and places his hands upon her shoulders.
	5—8	Each man peeps four times over his partner's shoulders, alternately to right and left, upon the first beat of each bar.
	9—10	All fall back to places (sk.s.).
	11—12	All turn single.

NEW BO-PEEP; or, PICKADILLA—*continued.*

MUSIC.		MOVEMENTS.
		FIRST PART—*continued.*
B2	1—2	Men turn, face the left wall, and move forward a double (small running steps).
	3—4	Women follow them and stand each behind her partner, placing her hands upon his shoulders (sk.s.).
	5—8	Women peep over their partners' shoulders four times, as men did in B1.
	9—10	All fall back to places (sk.s).
	11—12	All turn single.
		SECOND PART.
A	1—4	Partners side (r.s.).
	5—8	That again.
B1	1—12	Same as B2 in First Part.
B2	1—12	Same as B1 in First Part.
		THIRD PART.
A	1—4	Partners arm with the right.
	5—8	Partners arm with the left.
B1 and B2		Same as in First Part.

STAINES MORRIS.

Longways for as many as will; in as many parts as there
are dancers (1st Ed., 1650)

| 1 | 2 | 3 | 4 | . . . . . |
| (1) | (2) | (3) | (4) | . . . . . |

MUSIC.		MOVEMENTS.

FIRST PART.

A	1—4	All lead up a double and fall back a double to places (r.s.).
	5—8	That again.
B	1—2	All face left wall and move forward a double (r.s.).
	3—4	All fall back a double to places and face front (r.s.).
C	1—4	Partners set and turn single.
	5—8	That again.

SECOND PART.
(Whole-set).

A	1—4	First man moves down the middle and stands before the last woman (r.s.).
	5—8	First man and last woman side.
B	1—2	Both set, holding and raising right hands.
	3—4	Same again, holding and raising left hands.

STAINES MORRIS—*continued.*

MUSIC.		MOVEMENTS.
		SECOND PART—*continued.*
C	Bar 1	First man crosses hands with last woman and turns her half round, counter-clockwise, so that her back is turned to him.
	Bar 2	Standing in this position, they salute.
	3—4	Same again, the man turning the woman completely round clockwise.
	5—8	First man leads last woman up the middle to the first place (sk.s.), the rest of the women moving down one place (progressive).
		It is suggested that the last section be performed in the following way:—
C	Bar 1	First man moves a single to the right.
	Bar 2	First man honours last woman.
	Bar 3	First man moves a single to the left.
	Bar 4	First man honours last woman.
	5—8	As above.]
		These two parts are repeated until the first man has brought his own partner to the top, when all will once again be in their original places.

AMARILLIS.

Longways for as many as will; in three parts (4th Ed., 1670).

1	2	3	4	•	•	•	•	•
(1)	(2)	(3)	(4)	•	•	•	•	•

MUSIC.		MOVEMENTS.
		FIRST PART.
A	1—4	All lead up a double and fall back a double to places (r.s.).
	5—8	That again.
B	1—4	Men set to their partners, and then fall back four small steps to places (r.s.).
	5—8	Each man takes right hands with his partner, and turns her once or twice round under his right arm, clockwise, and hands her back to her place.
		SECOND PART. (Duple minor-set.)
A	1—2	First woman crosses over into the second place on the men's side; and then first man crosses over into the second place on the women's side (r.s.).
	3—4	Second couple leads up into the first place (r.s.).
	5--6	Second woman crosses over into the second place on the men's side; and then second man crosses over into the second place on the women's side (r.s.).

AMARILLIS—*continued.*

MUSIC.		MOVEMENTS.
		SECOND PART—*continued.*
	7—8	First couple leads up into first place (r.s.).
B	1—2	First man and second woman change places (r.s.).
	3—4	Second man and first woman change places (r.s) (progressive).
	5—8	First and second couples hands-four, once round.
		THIRD PART. (Duple minor-set.)
A	1—2	Second couple leads up between first couple (w.s.).
	3—4	Second man, facing up, dances four slips toward left wall; while second woman dances four slips toward right wall.
	5—6	Second man and second woman fall back four steps (r.s.).
	7—8	Second man and second woman face front and move forward four steps to places (r.s.).
B	1—2	First couple leads down into second place (w.s.).
	3—4	First man and first woman cast up to places (r.s.).
	5—8	First couple casts off into second place, while second couple moves up into first place (progressive).

BLACK JACK.

Longways for as many as will; in four parts (4th Ed., 1670).

MUSIC.		MOVEMENTS.
		FIRST PART.
A	1—4	All lead up a double and fall back a double to places (r.s.).
	5—8	That again.
B	1—4	Partners set and fall back from each other four small steps (r.s.).
	5—8	That again.
		SECOND PART.
		(Duple minor-set.)
A1	1—4	First man turns outward to his left and, followed by second woman, casts down below second man and moves up the middle to his place, second woman returning to her place (r.s.).
	5—8	First woman turns outward to her right and, followed by second man, casts down below second woman, and then moves up the middle to her place, second man returning to his place (r.s.).

BLACK JACK—*continued.*

MUSIC.		MOVEMENTS.
		SECOND PART—*continued.*
B1	1—4	First couple leads down the middle and back again.
	5—6	First couple casts down into the second place, second couple moving up into first place (r.s.) (progressive).
	7—8	First man and first woman set.
		THIRD PART.
		(Duple minor-set.)
A1	1—4	First man moves forward between first and second women. All three face right wall, take hands, move forward a double and fall back a double to places (r.s.).
	5—6	First and second men face left wall, take hands, move forward a double and fall back a double to places (r.s.).
B1	1—2	First and second couples hands-four, half-way round.
	3—4	Partners set.
	5—6	First and second couples hands-four, half-way round, counter-clockwise, to places.
	7—8	First couple casts down into second place, second couple moving up into first place (r.s.) (progressive).

BLACK JACK—*continued.*

MUSIC.		MOVEMENTS.
		FOURTH PART. (Duple minor-set.)
A1	1—4	First man and first woman cast down, meet below second man and second woman, and stand between them (r.s.).
	5—8	All four face up, take hands, move forward a double, and fall back a double (r.s.), first couple into the second place, and second couple into the first (progressive).
B1	1—4	First man turns his partner; while second man and woman set.
	5—8	Second man turns his partner; while the other two set.

JAMAICA.

Longways for as many as will; in two parts (4th Ed., 1670).

MUSIC.	MOVEMENTS.
	FIRST PART.
	(Duple minor-set.)
A1 1—4	First man and first woman cross hands, clasping right hands on the first beat of the first bar, and left hands on the first beat of the second bar, move half-way round a small circle, clockwise, and change places (sl.s.).
5—8	First man changes places with second woman in like manner; while second man does the same with first woman (progressive; improper*).
B1 1—8	First man and first woman fall back two small steps, and then go the Figure-Eight round second couple, the first man crossing over, passing counter-clockwise round second man and clockwise round second woman, the first woman crossing over passing clockwise round second woman and counter-clockwise round second man (sk.s.).

* In the next round the first couple will be proper, the second couple improper. Couples will be alternately proper and improper throughout the movement. If on their wrong sides, partners should change places when neutral.

JAMAICA—*continued.*

MUSIC.		MOVEMENTS.

SECOND PART.

(Duple minor-set.)

Partners, who are on their wrong sides, change places.

A1   1—4   First man turns second woman.

     5—8   Second man turns first woman.

B1   1—4   First man turns second man once-and a-half round and changes places with him; while first woman does the same with the second woman (progressive).

     5—8   First and second men turn their partners.

MY LADY CULLEN.

Longways for as many as will; in three parts (1st Ed., 1650).

| 1 | 2 | 3 | 4 | . . . ◂ . |

| (1) | (2) | (3) | (4) | . . . ◂ . |

MUSIC.		MOVEMENTS.

FIRST PART.

A1 1—4 | All lead up a double an' fall back a double to places (r.s.).

5—8 | That again.

B1 1—4 | Partners set and turn single.

5—8 | That again.

SECOND PART.

(Duple minor-set.)

A1 1—4 | First man and first woman cross over, cast down outside second woman and second man, respectively, cross over again and stand between second man and second woman, the first man on the left of the first woman (r.s.).

5—8 | First and second couples, four abreast, face up, take hands, move forward a double and back a double (r.s.), first couple falling into second place, and second couple into first place (progressive).

MY LADY CULLEN—*continued.*

MUSIC.		MOVEMENTS.
		SECOND PART—*continued.*
B1	1—4	Right-hands-across with first and second couples (r.s.).
	5—8	Left-hands-across with first and second couples (r.s.).
		THIRD PART.
		(Duple minor-set.)
A1	1—4	First man and first woman cast down and move up between second couple (r.s.).
	5—8	Second man and second woman cast up into the first place, while first couple moves down into second place (r.s.) (progressive).
B1	1—4	Second man and second woman face and take both hands, while first man and first woman do the same. Both couples then dance four slips up and four slips back again.
	5—8	Partners set and turn single.
		FOURTH PART.
		(Duple minor-set.)
A1	1—8	Same as in Second Part (progressive).
B1	1—4	Partners face and clap hands on the first beat of the first bar. First and second women arm with the right; while first and second men do the same.
	5—8	Partners arm with the left.

LONDON IS A FINE TOWN; OR,
WATTON TOWN'S END.

Longways for as many as will; in four parts (3rd Ed., 1665).

| 1 | 2 | 3 | 4 | • • • • • |
| (1) | (2) | (3) | (4) | • • • • • |

MUSIC.		MOVEMENTS.
		FIRST PART.
A1	1—4	All lead up a double and fall back a double to places (r.s.).
	5—6	All jump three times, facing their partners, on the two beats of bar 5 and the first beat of the following bar.
	7—8	All turn single.
A2	1—8	All that again.
		SECOND PART. (Duple minor-set.)
A1	1—4	First and second men fall back a double, and move forward a double to places; while first and second women do the same (r.s.).
	5—6	First and second men and their partners jump three times as before.
	7—8	First couple casts down into second place, while second couple moves up into first place (r.s.) (progressive).

LONDON IS A FINE TOWN; or,
WATTON TOWN'S END—*continued.*

MUSIC.		MOVEMENTS.
		THIRD PART.
		(Duple minor-set.)
A1	1—2	First man and second woman cross over and change places (r.s.).
	3—4	First woman and second man cross over and change places (r.s.).
	5—6	First and second men and their partners jump three times as before.
	7—8	First and second men change places with their partners (r.s.) (progressive).
		FOURTH PART.
		(Duple minor-set.)
A1	1—4	First and second couples hands-four, half-way round.
	5—6	First and second men and their partners jump three times as before.
	7—8	First and second men change places with their partners (r.s.) (progressive).

THE TWENTY-NINTH OF MAY.

Longways for as many as will; in three parts (7th Ed., 1686).

MUSIC.	MOVEMENTS.
	FIRST PART.
	(Duple minor-set.)
A1 1—8	First and second couples whole-pousette (r.s.) (Fig. 6, p. 45).
B1 Bar 1	First man and second woman change places (r.s.).
Bar 2	Second man and first woman change places (r.s.).
Bar 3	First and second couples hands-four two slips clockwise.
4—6	Same couples hands-four six slips, counter-clockwise, to places.
7—8	First couple casts down into second place, while second couple moves up into first place (r.s.) (progressive).
	SECOND PART.
	(Duple minor-set.)
A1 1—4	First man and second woman fall back two small steps, and then dance back-to-back, to places (r.s.).
5—8	Second man and first woman do the same.

THE TWENTY-NINTH OF MAY—*continued.*

MUSIC.		MOVEMENTS.
		SECOND PART—*continued.*
B1	1—6	First and second couples hands-four once-and-a-half round, men falling on the women's side, and women on the men's, and first couple below second couple.
	7—8	Partners cross over and change places (progressive).
		THIRD PART.
		(Duple minor set.)
A1	1—4	First man and first woman cross over, cast down, meet below the second couple, move up between second couple and stand, side by side, facing up (r.s.).
	5—8	Second man, first woman, first man, and second woman, four abreast, face up, take hands, move forward a double, and fall back a double (r.s.).
B1	Bar 1	First and second men honour, respectively, second and first women.
	Bar 2	First and second men honour their partners.
	3—4	First man turns second woman; while second man turns first woman.
	5—8	First and second men turn their partners, first couple falling into second place and second couple into first place (progressive).